bill cooks for kids

bill cooks for kids

NO-FUSS FOOD FOR
THE WHOLE FAMILY

Photography by Petrina Tinslay

Bill Granger

MURDOCH BOOKS

CONTENTS

Breakfast is my favourite meal of the day. Many people sacrifice breakfast in the struggle to keep up with the fast pace of life. But I always make an effort to have breakfast with my family. When we're rushed, which seems to be quite often in our crazy household, our standby breakfast is the homemade muesli I keep in the pantry for just such occasions, served with fresh fruit and yoghurt. Midweek breakfasts have to be quick and, with five of us round the table, toast — by the time it's buttered and I've found everyone's favourite topping — can be a bit of a bore.

We usually all decide on our breakfast, whether it be buckwheat pancakes or soft-boiled eggs or whatever, and we all share in its preparation while getting ready for the day. As far as I can see, if you eat a good breakfast you've done a third of your day's work for eating well.

BREAKFAST

VANILLA RICE PORRIDGE WITH CARAMELISED BANANAS

SERVES 4

1 litre (35 fl oz/4 cups) milk

55 g (2 oz/¼ cup) caster (superfine) sugar

1 teaspoon vanilla bean paste

180 g (6½ oz) arborio rice

2 bananas, thickly sliced on the diagonal

1 tablespoon brown sugar, plus extra to serve

1 tablespoon butter, cut into small pieces

Put the milk, sugar and vanilla bean paste in a large saucepan and bring to a simmer over medium heat. Add the rice and cook for 30 minutes, or until the rice is tender, stirring occasionally to stop it sticking to the pan. Remove from the heat and leave for 5 minutes.

Meanwhile, preheat the grill (broiler) to high. Put the banana in a shallow baking dish, sprinkle with the sugar and dot with the butter. Grill (broil) for 2–3 minutes, or until golden and caramelised.

To serve, spoon the rice pudding into bowls, top with banana and sprinkle with a little extra sugar.

MIX-AND-GO MUESLI

SERVES 8-12

400 g (14 oz/4 cups) rolled (porridge) oats

220 g (7¾ oz/2 cups) rolled barley

75 g (2¾ oz/1 cup) bran cereal

100 g (3½ oz/⅔ cup) almonds, chopped

55 g (2 oz/⅓ cup) sunflower seeds

70 g (2½ oz/½ cup) pepitas (pumpkin seeds)

80 g (2¾ oz/⅔ cup) dried pear, chopped

80 g (2¾ oz/⅔ cup) dried strawberries

Mix together all the ingredients and store in an airtight container.

Serve with milk or fresh berries and yoghurt.

"When fresh peaches are out of season you can use dried peaches or other dried fruit by soaking them in boiling water for 5 minutes."

FIVE-GRAIN PORRIDGE WITH BROWN SUGAR PEACHES

SERVES 4

250 g (9 oz/2½ cups) of mixed grains
   such as rolled (porridge) oats,
   rolled rice, rolled barley, triticale
   or kibbled rye (see Note)
625 ml (21½ fl oz/2½ cups) boiling
   water
625 ml (21½ fl oz/2½ cups) milk
3 peaches, quartered
75 g (2½ oz/⅓ cup firmly packed)
   brown sugar

TO SERVE
brown sugar, extra
warmed milk

Preheat the oven to 200°C (400°F/Gas 6).

Place the grains and boiling water in a saucepan and stir to combine. Leave for 10 minutes, then stir in the milk. Place over medium heat and slowly bring to the boil. Reduce the heat and simmer for 10 minutes, stirring often.

Meanwhile, place the peaches on a baking tray and sprinkle with the sugar. Bake for 15 minutes, or until the fruit has softened and slightly caramelised.

Spoon the porridge into serving bowls and top with the peaches. Serve with extra sugar and a jug of warmed milk.

NOTE
Some health food shops sell a five-grain mix which I think is ideal for this porridge. Triticale is an interesting grain – a cross between rye and wheat, with a delicious nutty flavour. Make up more than you need of the grain mix and store in an airtight container for up to 2 months.

BUTTERMILK PANCAKES

SERVES 4–6

250 g (9 oz/2 cups) plain
(all-purpose) flour

3 teaspoons baking powder

2 tablespoons sugar

2 eggs, lightly beaten

750 ml (26 fl oz/3 cups) buttermilk

75 g (2½ oz) unsalted butter, melted,
plus extra for greasing

TO SERVE

caramelised plums (see Note)

maple syrup

yoghurt

Stir the flour, baking powder, sugar and a pinch of salt together in a bowl. Add the eggs, buttermilk and melted butter and whisk to combine.

Heat a large non-stick frying pan over medium heat and brush a small portion of butter over the base. For each pancake, ladle 80 ml (2½ fl oz/⅓ cup) of batter into the pan and cook for about 2 minutes, until bubbles appear on the surface. Turn the pancakes over and cook for another minute. Transfer to a plate and keep warm while cooking the rest of the pancakes. The mixture makes 16 pancakes.

Serve the pancakes in stacks with caramelised plums, a jug of maple syrup and some yoghurt.

NOTE

To caramelise plums, cut the plums in half, remove the stones, then sprinkle the cut sides with sugar. Put the plums in a hot frying pan, cut side down. Sear the plums until the sugar melts and caramelises. This should take about a minute.

"What is it about French toast that brings out the child in all of us?"

FRENCH TOAST WITH FRESH BERRY SAUCE

SERVES 4

3 eggs
185 ml (6 fl oz/¾ cup) milk
8 thick slices brioche or panettone
30 g (1 oz) unsalted butter

FRESH BERRY SAUCE

250 g (9 oz/2 cups) raspberries
   or mixed berries
60 g (2¼ oz/¼ cup) caster
   (superfine) sugar
1 tablespoon lemon juice

TO SERVE

icing (confectioners') sugar,
   for sprinkling

Whisk the eggs and milk together in a bowl. Place the brioche or panettone in a shallow dish and pour the milk mixture over the top. Allow the milk to soak in thoroughly, then turn the bread over and soak the other side — if you are using panettone it will need to be soaked for a little longer because it is drier.

Heat a large non-stick frying pan over medium–high heat and melt half the butter. Add four slices of bread to the pan and fry for about 1 minute, until golden. Turn over and cook until the other side is golden. Repeat with the remaining bread.

Meanwhile, to make the berry sauce, put half the berries in a blender with the sugar and lemon juice and purée until smooth. Pour into a bowl, add the remaining berries and stir to combine.

Serve the French toast immediately with the berry sauce and a sprinkling of icing sugar.

RASPBERRY AND FIG SMOOTHIE

SERVES 2

125 g (4½ oz/1 cup) fresh raspberries
2 ripe figs, chopped
125 ml (4 fl oz/½ cup) natural yoghurt
125 ml (4 fl oz/½ cup) milk
2 teaspoons honey
a handful of ice cubes

Put all the ingredients in a blender and mix until smooth. Pour into two tall glasses and serve.

BANANA, STRAWBERRY AND ORANGE SMOOTHIE

SERVES 2

1 large ripe banana
150 g (5½ oz/1 cup) strawberries, hulled
250 ml (9 fl oz/1 cup) orange juice
a handful of ice cubes

Put all the ingredients in a blender and mix until smooth. Pour into two tall glasses and serve.

PINEAPPLE, HONEYDEW AND MINT SMOOTHIE

SERVES 2

160 g (5¾ oz/1 cup) chopped fresh pineapple
160 g (5¾ oz/1 cup) chopped honeydew melon
6 mint leaves
250 ml (9 fl oz/1 cup) pineapple juice
a handful of ice cubes

Put all the ingredients in a blender and mix until smooth. Pour into two tall glasses and serve.

BIRCHER MUESLI WITH PEAR AND BLUEBERRIES

SERVES 4

200 g (7 oz/2 cups) rolled (porridge) oats, or mixed rolled oats, barley and rye

375 ml (13 fl oz/1½ cups) pear juice

2 pears, skin left on and grated

125 g (4½ oz/½ cup) plain yoghurt

50 g (1¾ oz/⅓ cup) toasted chopped almonds (see Note)

80 g (2¾ oz/½ cup) blueberries

Put the grains in a bowl with the pear juice and leave to soak for 1 hour, or overnight, in the fridge.

Add the grated pear and yoghurt and mix well. Spoon the muesli into serving bowls and top each with toasted almonds and blueberries.

NOTE

The quickest and easiest way to toast nuts is to dry-fry them in a frying pan over medium heat. However, don't walk away from them because they burn very quickly.

FRIED EGGS

SERVES 1-2

2 teaspoons olive oil

2 eggs, at room temperature

Place a large non-stick frying pan over medium–high heat for 1 minute. Add the olive oil and swirl until the base of the pan is evenly coated. Carefully crack the eggs into the pan and sprinkle with sea salt and freshly ground black pepper. Cook for 1 minute. If you like the yolks of your eggs harder, cover the pan with a lid and cook for another minute.

SCRAMBLED EGGS

SERVES 2

2 eggs, at room temperature

80 ml (2½ fl oz/⅓ cup) cream

10 g (¼ oz) butter

Place the eggs, cream and a pinch of salt in a bowl and whisk together.

Melt the butter in a non-stick frying pan over high heat, then pour in the egg mixture and cook for 20 seconds, or until it begins to set around the edge. Using a wooden spoon, stir and bring the egg mixture on the edge of the pan into the centre. It is important to 'fold' the eggs, not scramble them. Leave for 20 seconds, then repeat the folding process.

When the eggs are just set, turn them out onto a plate and serve.

POACHED EGGS

SERVES 1-2

2 eggs, at room temperature

Fill a shallow frying pan with 5 cm (2 inches) water and place over high heat. Once the water boils, turn off the heat and break the eggs directly into the water, cracking the shells open at the water surface so the eggs simply slide into the water. Cover with a tight-fitting lid and leave to cook for 3 minutes, or until the egg whites are opaque. Remove from the pan with a slotted spoon and drain on a clean tea towel (dish towel).

BOILED EGGS

Place a saucepan of water over high heat and bring to the boil. Gently place your eggs, which should be at room temperature, into the water, then adjust the heat until the water is simmering.

For a soft-boiled egg, cook for 4 minutes; medium-boiled 5–6 minutes; and hard-boiled 10 minutes.

FRESH BAKED BEANS

SERVES 6

1 tablespoon olive oil

1 onion, finely chopped

100 g (3½ oz) pancetta, chopped

1 garlic clove, crushed

2 anchovies, chopped

1 teaspoon finely chopped thyme
  leaves

½ teaspoon dried oregano

400 g (14 oz) tin chopped tomatoes

2 x 400 g (14 oz) tins cannellini
  beans, rinsed

Preheat the oven to 160°C (315°F/Gas 2–3).

Heat the olive oil in a large flameproof casserole dish over medium heat. Add the onion and cook, stirring, for 5–6 minutes, or until the onion is soft. Add the pancetta and cook, stirring occasionally, for 5 minutes, or until slightly crisp. Add the garlic, anchovies, thyme and oregano and cook, stirring, for another minute.

Add the tomatoes and 125 ml (4 fl oz/½ cup) water. Bring to the boil, then reduce the heat and simmer for 10 minutes. Stir in the beans, put a lid on the casserole dish and bake in the oven for 30 minutes.

Season to taste with sea salt and freshly ground black pepper and serve.

"Breakfast is my favourite meal of the day, partly because it's the only meal you can justify eating in bed."

CHORIZO, POTATO AND CAPSICUM FRITTATA

SERVES 4

1½ tablespoons olive oil

1 chorizo sausage, sliced

1 red-skinned potato, diced

1 small onion, diced

1 red capsicum (pepper), diced

10 eggs

2 tablespoons chopped flat-leaf (Italian) parsley

2 tablespoons finely grated parmesan

Heat 2 teaspoons of the olive oil in a 20 cm (8 inch) frying pan over medium–high heat. Add the chorizo and cook, stirring occasionally, for 5–6 minutes, or until crisp. Drain on kitchen paper.

Reduce the heat to medium and add the remaining oil to the pan. Add the potato and onion and cook, stirring occasionally, for 5 minutes, or until the onion is soft. Add the capsicum and cook for 5 minutes, then return the chorizo to the pan.

Meanwhile, preheat the grill (broiler) to high.

Whisk the eggs and pour them into the pan. Reduce the heat to low, cover the pan and cook until the eggs have almost set. Sprinkle with the parsley and parmesan and then cook under the grill for 3–4 minutes, or until the frittata is golden and puffed.

MILK &
COOKIES

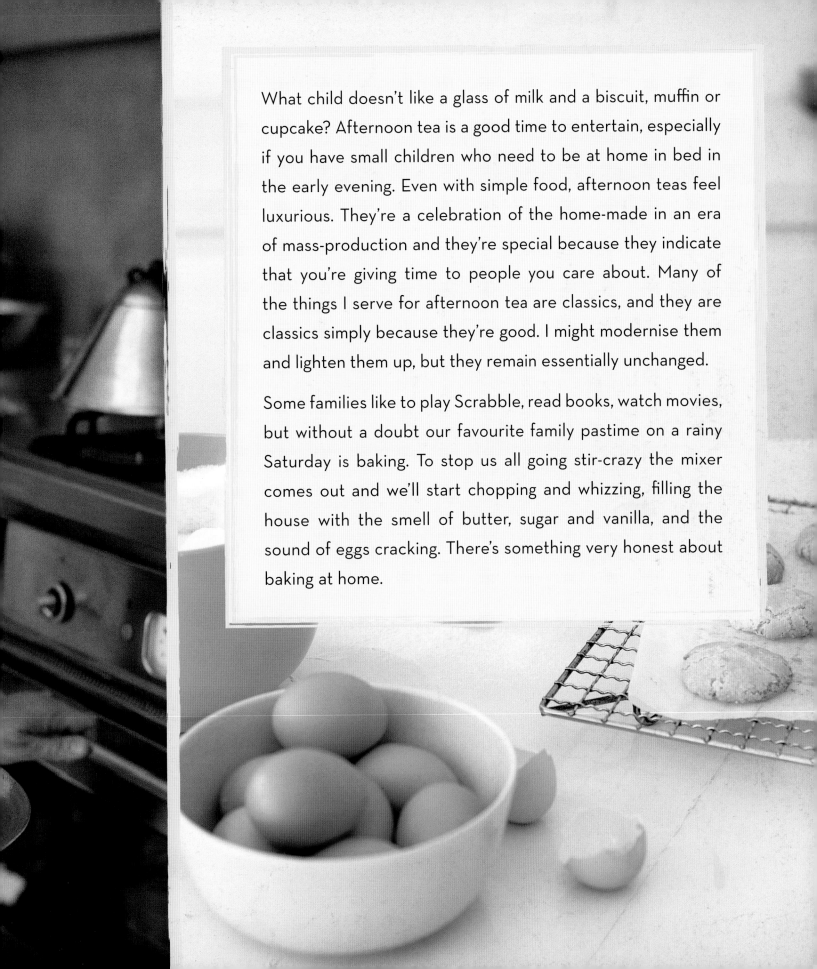

What child doesn't like a glass of milk and a biscuit, muffin or cupcake? Afternoon tea is a good time to entertain, especially if you have small children who need to be at home in bed in the early evening. Even with simple food, afternoon teas feel luxurious. They're a celebration of the home-made in an era of mass-production and they're special because they indicate that you're giving time to people you care about. Many of the things I serve for afternoon tea are classics, and they are classics simply because they're good. I might modernise them and lighten them up, but they remain essentially unchanged.

Some families like to play Scrabble, read books, watch movies, but without a doubt our favourite family pastime on a rainy Saturday is baking. To stop us all going stir-crazy the mixer comes out and we'll start chopping and whizzing, filling the house with the smell of butter, sugar and vanilla, and the sound of eggs cracking. There's something very honest about baking at home.

CHOC OATMEAL COOKIES

MAKES 30

150 g (5½ oz) unsalted butter, softened

220 g (7¾ oz/1 cup firmly packed) brown sugar

1 egg, lightly beaten

2 teaspoons vanilla extract

125 g (4½ oz/1 cup) plain (all-purpose) flour

1 teaspoon baking powder

225 g (8 oz/2⅓ cups) rolled (porridge) oats

170 g (6 oz/1 cup) chocolate chips

Preheat the oven to 180°C (350°F/Gas 4) and line three large baking trays with baking paper.

Cream the butter and sugar together in a bowl until fluffy and smooth. Add the egg and vanilla extract and beat until smooth. Sift the flour, baking powder and a pinch of salt into the bowl and mix lightly. Add the oats and chocolate chips and stir to combine.

Roll tablespoons of the mixture into balls and place on the baking trays. Flatten the balls with a fork dipped in flour. Bake the cookies for 20 minutes, or until pale golden.

Remove from the oven and cool on the trays for 5 minutes, before transferring the cookies to a wire rack to cool completely.

HOT CHOCOLATE

SERVES 4

75 g (2¾ oz/½ cup) good-quality
  chocolate melts (buttons)
1 litre (35 fl oz/4 cups) milk

Pour boiling water into four heatproof glasses and leave for 30 seconds to heat up the glasses.

Pour out the water and divide the chocolate buttons among the glasses. Hold each glass on its side and slowly turn it around so the chocolate melts and coats the side of the glass.

Warm the milk, pour into the glasses and serve.

MILKSHAKE

SERVES 2

500 ml (17 fl oz/2 cups) milk
2 scoops vanilla ice cream

CARAMEL SAUCE
100 g (3½ oz/½ cup lightly packed)
  brown sugar
250 ml (9 fl oz/1 cup) cream
1 teaspoon vanilla extract
15 g (½ oz) butter

Put all the caramel sauce ingredients in a small saucepan over medium heat and stir until the sauce comes to a slow boil. Cook, stirring carefully, for 5 minutes over low heat, or until thick and syrupy. Allow the sauce to cool.

Pour 4 tablespoons of the caramel sauce into a blender. Pour the remainder into an airtight jar and store it in the fridge to use another day.

Add the milk and cream to the blender and mix until smooth. Pour into two tall glasses and serve.

ICED JUMBLES

MAKES 20

60 g (2¼ oz) unsalted butter

230 g (8½ oz/⅔ cup)
   golden syrup

250 g (9 oz/2 cups) plain
   (all-purpose) flour

1 teaspoon bicarbonate of soda
   (baking soda)

1½ teaspoons ground ginger

1 teaspoon mixed spice
   (pumpkin pie spice)

ICING

1 egg white, lightly beaten

250 g (9 oz/2 cups) icing
   (confectioners') sugar

2 teaspoons lemon juice

a few drops of food colouring

Preheat the oven to 180°C (350°F/Gas 4) and line two baking trays with baking paper.

Stir the butter and golden syrup in a saucepan over medium heat until the butter has melted, then bring to the boil and remove from the heat. Leave to cool for 15 minutes.

Sift the flour, bicarbonate of soda and spices together, then stir into the syrup mixture.

Knead the dough on a lightly floured surface until smooth, then divide into four. Roll each portion into a 30 cm log and cut into 6 cm (2½ inch) lengths. Place on the tray and flatten each biscuit slightly. Bake for about 10 minutes, or until light golden. Cool on wire racks.

To make the icing, stir the egg white and icing sugar together until smooth. Add the lemon juice and food colouring and stir well. Spread the icing over the cooled biscuits.

GINGER BISCUITS WITH LEMON DRIZZLE ICING

MAKES ABOUT 20

250 g (9 oz/2 cups) plain (all-purpose) flour

1 teaspoon baking powder

1 teaspoon ground ginger

40 g (1½ oz/⅓ cup) icing (confectioners') sugar

70 g (2½ oz/⅓ cup) crystallised ginger, finely chopped

200 g (7 oz) unsalted butter, melted and cooled

1 teaspoon vanilla extract

LEMON DRIZZLE ICING

125 g (4½ oz/1 cup) icing (confectioners') sugar, sifted

1 tablespoon lemon juice

Preheat the oven to 180°C (350°F/Gas 4) and line two baking trays with baking paper.

Sift the flour, baking powder, ground ginger, icing sugar and a pinch of salt into a large mixing bowl.

Add the crystallised ginger and stir together. Add the butter and vanilla extract and, using a wooden spoon, stir until well combined.

Roll tablespoons of the dough into balls and set out on the baking trays, leaving enough room for the biscuits to spread. Lightly flatten the balls with a fork dipped in flour. Bake for 12–15 minutes, or until the biscuits are light golden. Leave on a wire rack to cool.

To make the icing, mix the icing sugar and lemon juice until smooth and glossy.

When the biscuits are completely cool, drizzle them with the icing.

PASSIONFRUIT MELTING MOMENTS

MAKES ABOUT 15

250 g (9 oz) unsalted butter, softened

60 g (2¼ oz/½ cup) icing (confectioners') sugar

225 g (8 oz/1¾ cups) plain (all-purpose) flour

85 g (3 oz/⅔ cup) cornflour (cornstarch)

PASSIONFRUIT CREAM

60 g (2¼ oz) unsalted butter, softened

125 g (4½ oz/1 cup) icing (confectioners') sugar, sifted

1 tablespoon passionfruit pulp

Preheat the oven to 170°C (325°F/Gas 3) and line two large baking trays with baking paper.

Cream the butter and sugar until pale and creamy. Sift together the flour and cornflour, add to the butter mixture and beat well. (Alternatively, mix the sugar, flour and cornflour in a food processor, pulsing until combined. Add the softened butter and process until the mixture comes together.)

Using floured hands, take scant tablespoons of the mixture and roll it into balls. Place on the baking trays and flatten slightly with a fork dipped in flour. Bake for 15–18 minutes, or until the biscuits are light golden, then cool on a wire rack.

To make the passionfruit cream, beat the butter using electric beaters until completely smooth. Gradually add the icing sugar and continue beating until pale and creamy. Add the passionfruit pulp and beat well.

Join the cooled biscuits together with dollops of the passionfruit cream.

"My auntie (a real old-fashioned country biscuit-maker) made the best melting moments. This is her recipe, although without the custard powder she liked to add. They might not be quite as yellow, but they're just as delicious."

HEART SHORTBREAD KISSES

MAKES 15 DOUBLE SHORTBREAD KISSES

40 g (1½ oz/⅓ cup) icing (confectioners') sugar, sifted, plus extra for dusting

250 g (9 oz) unsalted butter, softened

1 teaspoon vanilla extract

60 g (2¼ oz/½ cup) cornflour (cornstarch)

185 g (6½ oz/1½ cups) plain (all-purpose) flour

85 g (3 oz/¼ cup) raspberry jam

Beat the icing sugar and butter together in a bowl until just combined. Add the vanilla extract, sifted cornflour and flour and a pinch of salt, then mix until a dough forms. Mould into a log 6 cm (2½ inches) in diameter, wrap in plastic wrap and refrigerate for 30 minutes.

Preheat the oven to 180°C (350°F/Gas 4). Grease two large baking trays and line with baking paper.

Remove the dough from the fridge and cut into 7 mm (⅜ inch) slices, then cut out shapes using a 5 cm (2 inch) heart-shaped cutter. Reroll the excess dough and repeat the process until all the dough is used up.

Place the biscuits on the baking trays and bake for 15–20 minutes, or until golden brown. Transfer to wire racks and leave to cool completely.

Spread half the biscuits with the jam, top with the remaining biscuits and dust with extra icing sugar.

SULTANA SCONES

MAKES 12

1 tablespoon icing (confectioners')
   sugar

310 g (11 oz/2½ cups) plain
   (all-purpose) flour

1½ tablespoons baking powder

85 g (3 oz/½ cup) sultanas
   (golden raisins)

1 teaspoon grated orange zest

250 ml (9 fl oz/1 cup) milk

30 g (1 oz) unsalted butter, melted

TO SERVE

butter or whipped cream

raspberry jam

Preheat the oven to 220°C (425°F/Gas 7). Grease a baking tray.

Sift the icing sugar, flour, baking powder and a pinch of salt into a bowl. Add the sultanas and orange zest and stir to combine. Add the milk and butter and stir with a knife to combine. Knead quickly but lightly until smooth, handling the dough as little as possible. Press out on a floured surface to about 3 cm (1¼ inches) thick.

Use a cutter or glass to cut out 5 cm (2 inch) rounds. Place close together on the baking tray. Gather the scraps together, knead again and cut out more rounds.

Bake for 10 minutes, or until the scones are puffed and golden. Serve with butter or whipped cream, topped with jam.

"When whipping cream, take care not to overwhip. The cream should still be quite soft and wet, not firm and dry."

MANGO LASSI

MAKES 1

130 g (4¾ oz/½ cup) plain yoghurt
125 ml (4 fl oz/½ cup) orange juice
1 mango, cubed
3 large ice cubes

Place all the ingredients in a blender and mix until the mango is well combined. Pour into a tall glass and serve.

RASPBERRY AND STRAWBERRY SMOOTHIE

MAKES 1

4 strawberries, hulled
30 g (1 oz/¼ cup) raspberries
15 g (½ oz) plain yoghurt
125 ml (4 fl oz/½ cup) milk
3-4 large ice cubes

Place all the ingredients in a blender and mix until smooth. Pour into a tall glass and serve.

"Like many a budding cook, I tackled baking first when I started experimenting in the kitchen as a child and today I still feel a little of that seven-year-old boy's wonder."

BANANA MAPLE UPSIDE-DOWN CAKE

SERVES 8-10

100 g (3½ oz) unsalted butter,
  softened
220 g (7¾ oz/1 cup) caster
  (superfine) sugar
4 eggs
1 teaspoon vanilla extract
155 g (5½ oz/1¼ cups) plain
  (all-purpose) flour
1 teaspoon baking powder

CARAMEL TOPPING

50 g (1¾ oz) unsalted butter
60 g (2¼ oz/¼ cup firmly packed)
  brown sugar
60 ml (2 fl oz/¼ cup) maple syrup
3-4 bananas, sliced in half lengthways

TO SERVE

vanilla ice cream (optional)

Preheat the oven to 180°C (350°F/Gas 4).

Place the caramel topping ingredients in a small saucepan. Cook, stirring, over medium heat for 10 minutes, or until the sugar has dissolved and the syrup is rich and golden. Pour the syrup into a 23 cm (9 inch) greased or non-stick springform cake tin and arrange the sliced bananas, cut-side down, over the base of the tin.

Place the butter and sugar in a bowl and beat until pale and creamy. Add the eggs one at a time, beating after each addition, then add the vanilla extract.

Sift the flour, baking powder and a pinch of salt, then gently fold through the butter mixture. Spoon the batter evenly over the bananas and smooth the top with a spatula.

Place the cake on a baking tray to catch any escaping syrup and bake for 35 minutes, or until a skewer inserted into the centre of the cake comes out clean.

Remove from the oven and leave in the tin for 5 minutes to cool slightly. Transfer to a large serving plate. Serve warm, with vanilla ice cream if desired.

NOTE

This recipe can also be made very successfully with granny smith apples. Cook the sliced apples in the caramel topping mixture for 5 minutes, before placing in the tin and topping with the cake mixture.

ALMOND BISCUITS

MAKES 30

320 g (11¼ oz/2 cups) blanched
  almonds

3 egg whites

330 g (11¾ oz/1½ cups) caster
  (superfine) sugar

40 g (1½ oz/⅓ cup) plain
  (all-purpose) flour, plus
  2 teaspoons sugar,
  for sprinkling

Preheat the oven to 180°C (350°F/Gas 4). Grease a
baking tray and line with baking paper.

Finely grind the almonds in a food processor. Beat the
egg whites until stiff peaks form, then fold the ground
almonds into the egg whites. Mix in the sugar and all
the flour.

Roll tablespoons of the dough into balls and place on
the baking tray. Sprinkle with extra sugar and bake for
15 minutes, or until golden. Leave to cool on a wire rack.

COCONUT MACAROONS

MAKES 20

2 egg whites

110 g (3¾ oz/½ cup) caster
  (superfine) sugar

130 g (4¾ oz/2 cups) shredded
  coconut

95 g (3¼ oz/¾ cup) roughly chopped
  macadamia nuts

1 teaspoon grated lime zest

Preheat the oven to 160°C (315°F/Gas 2–3) and line
two large baking trays with baking paper.

Mix all the ingredients together in a bowl (you may need
to use your hands).

Shape tablespoons of the mixture into mounds on the
baking trays. Bake for 10–15 minutes, or until light
golden brown. Leave to cool on the trays.

*"I sometimes serve coconut
macaroons as a dessert with a
scoop of coconut ice cream."*

DOuBLE CHOC-CHIP COOKIES

MAKES ABOUT 30

250 g (9 oz) unsalted butter,
   softened

350 g (12 oz) brown sugar

1 teaspoon vanilla extract

2 eggs, lightly beaten

310 g (11 oz/2½ cups) plain
   (all-purpose) flour

55 g (2 oz/½ cup) cocoa powder

2 teaspoons baking powder

2 teaspoons sea salt

350 g (12 oz) dark chocolate,
   chopped

Preheat the oven to 180°C (350°F/Gas 4). Grease two large baking trays and line with baking paper.

Beat together the butter and sugar until light and creamy. Add the vanilla extract and eggs and stir together well.

Sift in the flour, cocoa powder, baking powder and salt and mix until just combined. Fold in the chocolate.

Place large spoonfuls of the mixture on the baking trays, leaving room for spreading. Bake for 15–20 minutes, or until the bases are cooked. Leave to cool on the trays.

APRICOT BARS

MAKES 24

155 g (5½ oz/1¼ cups) plain
  (all-purpose) flour

100 g (3½ oz/½ cup lightly packed)
  brown sugar

110 g (3¾ oz/½ cup) caster
  (superfine) sugar

1 teaspoon baking powder

175 g (6 oz) unsalted butter, chilled
  and diced, plus 40 g (1½ oz) melted
  unsalted butter, for drizzling

100 g (3½ oz/1 cup) rolled
  (porridge) oats

90 g (3¼ oz/1 cup) desiccated
  coconut

325 g (11½ oz/2½ cups) chopped
  dried apricots

115 g (4 oz/⅓ cup) apricot jam

Preheat the oven to 180°C (350°F/Gas 4). Lightly grease a 20 x 30 cm (8 x 12 inch) baking tin and line with baking paper.

Mix the flour, brown sugar, caster sugar, baking powder, butter and 2 pinches of salt in a food processor until a dough forms, or rub the ingredients together in a bowl with your fingertips. Mix in the oats and coconut. Reserve a cupful of dough and press the remainder evenly into the baking tin. Bake for 15 minutes, or until golden.

Put the apricots and 125 ml (4 fl oz/½ cup) water in a small saucepan over low heat and cook, stirring occasionally, until the liquid has been absorbed. Cool slightly, then spoon the mixture over the dough base. Dot the jam over the apricots and crumble the reserved dough over the top. Drizzle with the melted butter.

Bake for 30–35 minutes, or until the topping is lightly golden. Leave to cool completely in the tray. Slice into squares and store in an airtight container.

PINK LEMONADE

SERVES 6

110 g (3¾ oz/½ cup) caster
  (superfine) sugar
250 ml (9 fl oz/1 cup) cranberry juice
250 ml (9 fl oz/1 cup) lemon juice
750 ml (26 fl oz/3 cups) chilled
  soda water

Put the sugar and 125 ml (4 fl oz/½ cup) water in a saucepan and stir over low heat until the sugar has dissolved. Remove from the heat and leave to cool.

Mix the sugar syrup with the cranberry juice, lemon juice and soda water and stir together well.

CRANBERRY AND WHITE CHOCOLATE COOKIES

MAKES 30

150 g (5½ oz) unsalted butter,
  softened
165 g (5¾ oz/¾ cup firmly packed)
  brown sugar
1 egg, lightly beaten
2 teaspoons vanilla extract
125 g (4½ oz/1 cup) plain
  (all-purpose) flour
1 teaspoon baking powder
200 g (7 oz/2 cups) rolled
  (porridge) oats
140 g (5 oz/1 cup) white chocolate
  chunks
85 g (3 oz/⅔ cup) dried cranberries

Preheat the oven to 180°C (350°F/Gas 4) and line three baking trays with baking paper.

Cream the butter and sugar together until pale and creamy. Add the egg and vanilla extract and beat until smooth.

Sift the flour, baking powder and a pinch of salt into a bowl. Add the oats, chocolate and cranberries and stir together, then add to the butter mixture and stir together well.

Roll small tablespoons of the mixture into balls and place on the baking trays. Flatten the balls with a fork dipped in flour. Bake for 12–15 minutes, or until pale golden. Leave to cool on the trays for 5 minutes before transferring to a wire rack to cool completely.

"I want my family to grow up with good memories around food...nothing makes me feel happier than filling the house with the warm aroma of freshly baked cakes."

LAMINGTONS

MAKES 16

6 eggs
150 g (5½ oz/⅔ cup) caster
  (superfine) sugar
200 g (7 oz/1⅔ cups) self-raising
  flour
30 g (1 oz) unsalted butter, melted
360 g (12¾ oz/4 cups) desiccated
  coconut

CHOCOLATE ICING
500 g (1 lb 2 oz/4 cups) icing
  (confectioners') sugar
200 g (7 oz) dark chocolate, chopped
15 g (½ oz) unsalted butter
125 ml (4 fl oz/½ cup) milk

Preheat the oven to 180°C (350°F/Gas 4). Lightly grease and line the base of an 18 x 28 cm (7 x 11 inch) cake tin with baking paper.

Beat the eggs for about 5 minutes using electric beaters until light and fluffy. Gradually add the sugar and continue beating until the mixture is thick and the sugar has dissolved. Sift in the flour, then fold in lightly. Add the butter and 3 tablespoons hot water and stir gently to combine. Pour into the cake tin and bake for 30 minutes, or until the sponge is golden. Cool on a wire rack.

Put the chocolate icing ingredients in a heatproof bowl and place over a saucepan of simmering water. Stir constantly until well combined and smooth.

Cut the sponge into 16 squares. Put the coconut in a bowl. Dip each sponge square into the chocolate icing, then in the coconut.

Leave on a wire rack to dry completely before serving.

CRUNCHY-TOP PEAR MUFFINS

MAKES 6

125 g (4½ oz/1 cup) plain
  (all-purpose) flour

60 g (2¼ oz/½ cup) wholemeal
  (whole-wheat) plain
  (all-purpose) flour

3 teaspoons baking powder

2 teaspoons ground cinnamon

100 g (3½ oz/1 cup) rolled
  (porridge) oats

150 g (5½ oz/¾ cup lightly packed)
  brown sugar

2 eggs

260 g (9¼ oz/1 cup) low-fat yoghurt

125 ml (4 fl oz/½ cup) grapeseed oil
  (or other light-flavoured oil)

1 pear, peeled and diced

40 g (1½ oz/⅓ cup) pecan nuts,
  finely chopped

Preheat the oven to 180°C (350°F/Gas 4). Line six 250 ml (9 fl oz/1 cup) muffin holes with paper cases, or just grease them well.

Sift the flours, baking powder and cinnamon into a large bowl. Add the oats and all but 3 tablespoons of the sugar and stir together. Make a well in the centre.

Whisk together the eggs, yoghurt and oil. Pour into the well in the dry ingredients and stir until just combined. Fold the pear through, being careful not to overmix. Spoon into the muffin cases.

Mix the pecans with the remaining sugar. Sprinkle over the muffins and bake for 20–25 minutes, or until golden brown.

REAL MUESLI BARS

MAKES 16

350 g (12 oz/3½ cups) rolled (porridge) oats
35 g (1¼ oz/½ cup) shredded coconut
50 g (1¾ oz/½ cup) flaked almonds
40 g (1½ oz/½ cup) wheatgerm
40 g (1½ oz/¼ cup) sesame seeds
40 g (1½ oz/¼ cup) sunflower seeds
55 g (2 oz/⅓ cup) chopped dried apricots
260 g (9¼ oz/¾ cup) honey
60 g (2¼ oz/¼ cup firmly packed) brown sugar
125 ml (4 fl oz/½ cup) vegetable oil

Preheat the oven to 130°C (250°F/Gas 1). Lightly grease a 35 x 25 cm (14 x 10 inch) baking tin and line with baking paper.

Put the oats, coconut, almonds, wheatgerm, seasame seeds, sunflower seeds and apricots in a bowl.

Put the honey, sugar and oil in a small saucepan and stir over medium heat until the sugar has dissolved. Pour the mixture over the dry ingredients and stir until well combined, mixing with your hands if necessary.

Press the mixture into the baking tin and bake for 50 minutes, or until golden brown. Cut into bars while still warm.

PLAY-DATE DINNERS

I'm not really a fan of making special meals for children. I always give the girls food that we like to eat, for purely selfish reasons: like most parents I don't want to cook twice in an evening. But sometimes it's good to get the kids fed early, so I do have a few stand-bys for very simple kiddy dinners — and I admit that sometimes these become our dinner as well! I try to keep meals as pure and balanced as possible, serving a range of different foods. If you find your kids don't eat something, keep serving it and don't make a big deal about it. Spoil your family with fresh food, not processed treats. Forget designer clothes or expensive toys — the most important gift we can give our children is a palate for good unadulterated food, which in turn can lead to a long, healthy life.

EGG NOODLES WITH TOFU AND GREEN BEANS

SERVES 4

375 g (13 oz) fresh egg noodles

2 tablespoons soy sauce

1 tablespoon lime juice

1 tablespoon fish sauce

2 teaspoons brown sugar

1 tablespoon light-flavoured oil
(such as canola)

4 cm (1½ inch) piece of fresh ginger,
peeled, julienned or grated

200 g (7 oz) green beans, sliced
on the diagonal

300 g (10½ oz) tofu, cut into
long batons

TO SERVE

cucumber batons

chopped cashew nuts

Cook the noodles in boiling water according to the packet instructions. Drain and set aside.

Meanwhile, stir together the soy sauce, lime juice, fish sauce and sugar.

Heat a wok or large frying pan over high heat. Add the oil and, when smoking, add the ginger and beans and stir-fry for 2 minutes.

Add the tofu and stir-fry until golden. Add the soy sauce mixture and cook for 1 minute, or until slightly reduced.

Add the noodles to the wok and toss well, or divide the noodles among serving bowls and top with the sauce. Serve topped with the cucumber and cashews.

"The sweetness of hoisin is perfect for young palates and a great intro to grown-up flavours."

STIR-FRIED PORK WITH HOISIN AND GREENS

SERVES 4

2 teaspoons cornflour (cornstarch)

1 tablespoon sesame oil

1 teaspoon Chinese five-spice

400 g (14 oz) pork leg steak,
    cut into thin strips

2 tablespoons soy sauce

2 tablespoons hoisin sauce

3 tablespoons chicken stock

1 tablespoon peanut oil

3 cm (1¼ inch) piece of fresh ginger,
    peeled and cut into thin strips

1 bunch broccolini, cut into
    long florets

6 spring onions (scallions), chopped

TO SERVE
steamed jasmine rice

Mix together the cornflour, sesame oil and five-spice. Put the pork in a non-metallic bowl, pour the cornflour mixture over the top and stir to coat. Cover and refrigerate for 20 minutes.

Mix together the soy sauce, hoisin sauce and stock. Heat the peanut oil in a large wok or large frying pan over high heat. Add the ginger, broccolini and spring onion and stir-fry for 2 minutes, or until the broccolini is just cooked. Remove from the wok.

Add the pork to the wok and stir-fry for 2–3 minutes, or until the pork is light golden. Return the vegetables to the wok, add the soy sauce mixture and stir-fry for 2 minutes.

Serve with jasmine rice.

RIGATONI AND CHICKEN BOLOGNESE

SERVES 4-6

2 tablespoons extra virgin olive oil

1 onion, chopped

1 celery stalk, finely chopped

2 garlic cloves, chopped

2 slices pancetta or prosciutto, chopped

500 g (1 lb 2 oz) minced (ground) chicken

375 ml (13 fl oz/1½ cups) tomato passata (puréed tomatoes)

500 g (1 lb 2 oz) rigatoni

3 tablespoons chopped flat-leaf (Italian) parsley

TO SERVE
grated parmesan cheese

Heat the olive oil in a saucepan over medium heat. Add the onion, celery and garlic and season with sea salt and freshly ground black pepper. Cook, stirring occasionally, for 7 minutes, or until the onion is golden.

Add the pancetta and chicken and stir constantly with a wooden spoon to break up any lumps. When the chicken is cooked through, add the passata and simmer for 10 minutes.

Meanwhile, cook the pasta in a large saucepan of boiling salted water until al dente. Drain.

Toss the pasta with the sauce and mix the parsley through. Serve sprinkled with parmesan.

PASTA BOWS WITH SPRING PEAS AND PROSCIUTTO

SERVES 2-4

1 tablespoon extra virgin olive oil

100 g (3½ oz) prosciutto, sliced

1 white onion, sliced

250 ml (9 fl oz/1 cup) chicken stock

200 g (7 oz/1⅓ cups) shelled fresh peas

500 g (1 lb 2 oz) farfalle

20 g (¾ oz) butter

230 g (8 oz/1 cup) fresh ricotta

Heat the olive oil in a saucepan over low heat. Cook the prosciutto until golden, then remove from the pan. Add the onion to the pan and cook until soft. Add the stock, bring to the boil, then cook until the stock has reduced by half. Add the peas and simmer gently for 3 minutes.

Meanwhile, cook the pasta in a large saucepan of boiling salted water until al dente. Drain well and add to the sauce with the butter.

Spoon into bowls, crumble the ricotta over the top and season with sea salt and freshly ground black pepper.

TOO-TIRED-TO-COOK PASTA WITH CHEESE

SERVES 2-4

500 g (1 lb 2 oz) pasta wheels

50 g (1¾ oz) butter

60 g (2¼ oz/½ cup) grated parmesan, plus extra for sprinkling

TO SERVE

2 tablespoons basil leaves

Cook the pasta in a large saucepan of boiling salted water until al dente. Drain well and return to the warm pan. Stir in the butter and parmesan and sprinkle with sea salt. Serve topped with extra parmesan and the basil.

"I don't know how we ever lived without pasta — it's such a quick and easy food to have in the pantry when you're feeding children. Buy a variety of shapes to keep them interested."

FISH FINGERS WITH FRIES

SERVES 4-6

80 g (2¾ oz/1 cup firmly packed)
   fresh breadcrumbs

60 g (2¼ oz/½ cup) grated parmesan

2 eggs, lightly beaten

60 g (2¼ oz/½ cup) plain
   (all-purpose) flour

500 g (1 lb 2 oz) firm white fish fillets
   (I like flathead), cut into fat strips

1 tablespoon olive oil

25 g (1 oz) butter

OVEN-BAKED FRIES

1.25 kg (2 lb 12 oz) potatoes,
   scrubbed but not peeled

3 teaspoons olive oil

TO SERVE

lemon wedges

caper mayonnaise (optional)

Preheat the oven to 230°C (450°F/Gas 8) and put two baking trays in the oven to heat up for 20 minutes.

To make the fries, cut the potatoes into chips, dry with a clean tea towel (dish towel), toss with the olive oil and sprinkle with sea salt. Remove the hot baking trays from the oven, lay a sheet of baking paper on each one, then spread the chips on top. Return the trays to the oven and bake the chips for 30 minutes, or until golden, turning with tongs halfway through cooking.

Meanwhile, mix the breadcrumbs and parmesan together in a bowl and season with sea salt and freshly ground black pepper. Put the eggs in another bowl. Mix the flour with some salt and pepper in a third bowl.

Dip each piece of fish in the flour, then the egg, then the breadcrumbs. (You can do this in advance if you like, and then keep the crumbed fish covered in the fridge for up to 2 hours.)

Heat the olive oil and butter in a large non-stick frying pan over medium–high heat. Add the fish in batches and cook gently for about 2 minutes on each side, until lightly golden, adding a little more oil and butter if needed.

Serve the fish fingers with the fries and lemon wedges, and perhaps a bowl of caper mayonnaise.

"Fish fingers, whether they're for kids or adults, are always great with caper mayonnaise. Just stir a few capers, some lemon juice and chopped flat-leaf (Italian) parsley through whole-egg mayonnaise."

NO-STIR TOMATO RISOTTO

SERVES 4-6

1 tablespoon olive oil

25 g (1 oz) butter

1 onion, finely chopped

250 g (9 oz) arborio rice

500 ml (17 fl oz/2 cups) chicken stock

250 ml (9 fl oz/1 cup) tomato passata
   (puréed tomatoes)

1 teaspoon sugar

2 tablespoons shredded basil leaves

Heat a large heavy-based saucepan over medium heat. Add the olive oil, butter and onion and season with sea salt. Cook until the onion is translucent, stirring occasionally. Add the rice and stir for a few minutes, until the grains glisten.

Increase the heat to high and add the stock, tomato passata and 375 ml (13 fl oz/1½ cups) boiling water. Bring to the boil, stirring occasionally.

Reduce the heat to low, then cover and cook for 15–20 minutes, or until the rice is tender. Remove from the heat, stir in the sugar and serve scattered with the basil.

SPLIT PEA SOUP

SERVES 4

3 tablespoons olive oil

3 leeks, white part only, chopped

4 garlic cloves, crushed

500 g (1 lb 2 oz/2¼ cups) dried
   green split peas, soaked
   overnight and drained

2 litres (70 fl oz/8 cups) chicken stock

TO SERVE

chopped flat-leaf (Italian) parsley

toasted ham and cheese sandwiches
   (see below)

Heat a large saucepan over medium heat. Add olive oil, leek and garlic and season with sea salt and freshly ground black pepper. Cook, stirring, until the leek becomes translucent.

Add the peas and stock and bring to the boil. Reduce the heat to low and simmer for 40 minutes, stirring occasionally and skimming any froth from the surface.

Ladle into serving bowls, sprinkle with parsley and serve with toasted ham and cheese sandwiches.

TOASTED HAM AND CHEESE SANDWICHES

SERVES 4

8 slices white sourdough bread

1 tablespoon dijon mustard

4 thick slices leg ham

4 slices gruyère or Swiss-style cheese

2 tablespoons olive oil

Spread four slices of bread with the mustard. Top with a slice of ham, then cheese, and season with sea salt and freshly ground black pepper. Add another slice of bread to make a sandwich.

Heat a large non-stick frying pan over medium heat. Add half the olive oil and swirl to cover the base of the pan. Put two sandwiches in the pan and put another frying pan on top to squash them down. (I often put a couple of tins in the top frying pan for extra weight, which makes the sandwiches nice and crisp.)

Cook for 1–2 minutes, or until golden underneath, then flip the sandwiches over, replace the weight and cook for a couple of minutes longer.

Cook the other two sandwiches in the remaining oil.

CHILLI BEAN BURRITOS WITH CORN SALSA

SERVES 4

1 tablespoon olive oil

1 onion, finely chopped

1 celery stalk, finely chopped

2 garlic cloves, crushed

1 long red chilli, finely chopped

a pinch of cayenne pepper

1 teaspoon ground coriander

1 teaspoon ground cumin

2 x 400 g (14 oz) tins chopped
   tomatoes

2 x 400 g (14 oz) tins red kidney
   beans, rinsed

juice of 1 lime

2 tablespoons chopped coriander
   (cilantro)

CORN SALSA

1½ tablespoons olive oil

300 g (10½ oz/1½ cups) corn
   kernels, cut from the cob

1 celery stalk, diced

4 spring onions (scallions), finely
   chopped

small handful coriander (cilantro)
   leaves

1 tablespoon lime juice

1 long green chilli, seeded and
   finely chopped

TO SERVE

warmed tortillas

natural yoghurt

Heat the olive oil in a large heavy-based saucepan over medium–low heat. Add the onion and celery and cook, stirring occasionally, for 6–7 minutes, or until the vegetables are slightly soft. Add the garlic, chilli and spices and cook, stirring, for 1–2 minutes, until fragrant.

Add the tomatoes and stir well. Add the kidney beans and bring to the boil, then reduce the heat to very low. Simmer, stirring frequently, for 15 minutes, or until the sauce is thick. Stir in the lime juice and coriander.

To make the corn salsa, heat 1 tablespoon of the olive oil in a large frying pan over high heat. Add the corn and cook, stirring frequently, for 3–4 minutes. Tip the corn into a large bowl and add the celery, spring onion, coriander, lime juice, chilli and remaining oil. Season with sea salt and freshly ground black pepper and mix together well.

Spoon some bean mixture down the middle of each tortilla, then wrap up firmly. Serve with the corn salsa and a dollop of yoghurt.

CRISPY POTATO CAKE

SERVES 4-6

750 g (1 lb 10 oz) all-purpose
potatoes, such as desiree

1 small onion

4 spring onions (scallions), finely
sliced

2 eggs, lightly beaten

2 teaspoons plain (all-purpose) flour

½ cup roughly chopped flat-leaf
(Italian) parsley

1 tablespoon olive oil

Peel the potatoes and onion. Grate the potatoes into a bowl, then the onion (this can be done in a food processor if you wish). Wrap them in a clean tea towel (dish towel) and squeeze out the excess moisture.

Place in a bowl with the spring onion, eggs, flour and parsley. Season with sea salt and freshly ground black pepper and stir to combine.

Preheat the grill (broiler) to its highest setting. Heat a 22 cm (9 inch) non-stick, ovenproof frying pan over medium heat and add the olive oil. When the oil is hot, add the potato mixture and spread it out so that it covers the base of the pan. Cover and cook for about 10 minutes, shaking the pan frequently to stop the potato sticking.

Heat the potato cake under the grill for 6–7 minutes, or until it is fully cooked and well browned. Once browned, turn the potato cake out onto a serving platter. Sprinkle with extra salt and pepper, cut into wedges and serve with a salad of your choice.

"As I get older and my life becomes busier with work and family, the time available to prepare and cook meals gets shorter. But being busier actually increases the desire to spend time connecting with home. Food's a big part of that."

HAM LASAGNE

SERVES 6

3 x 400 g (14 oz) tins chopped
   tomatoes

500 g (1 lb 2 oz/3⅓ cups) cherry
   tomatoes

3 garlic cloves, crushed

3 tablespoons olive oil

600 g (1 lb 5 oz) fresh lasagne sheets

12 thick slices leg ham

750 g (1 lb 10 oz/3¼ cups) fresh
   ricotta

450 g (1 lb) fresh mozzarella cheese
   or bocconcini (baby mozzarella),
   sliced

100 g (3½ oz/¾ cup) grated
   parmesan

TO SERVE
basil leaves

Preheat the oven to 180°C (350°F/Gas 4).

Put the tinned tomatoes and cherry tomatoes in a saucepan and bring to the boil. Reduce the heat to low and simmer for 20–25 minutes. Add the garlic, 2 tablespoons of the olive oil and a pinch of sea salt and cook for another minute.

Cut the lasagne sheets to fit a 25 x 35 cm (10 x 14 inch) baking dish. Lightly grease the dish with olive oil and spread with three tablespoons of the tomato sauce. Top with a sheet of pasta and then an eighth of the tomato sauce. Tear and scatter an eighth each of the ham, ricotta and mozzarella over the sauce. Repeat the layers until the pasta, sauce, ham and cheese have been used up. Sprinkle the parmesan and some salt and freshly ground black pepper over the top and drizzle with the remaining oil.

Cover with foil and bake for 20 minutes. Remove the foil and bake for another 30 minutes, or until the top is golden brown. Serve garnished with basil leaves.

SAUSAGES WITH WHOLEMEAL FUSILLI

SERVES 4

1 tablespoon olive oil

4 Italian-style sausages

1 red onion, cut into wedges

1 red capsicum (pepper),
   roughly chopped

2 garlic cloves, crushed

2 x 400 g (14 oz) tins chopped
   tomatoes

½ teaspoon chilli flakes

1 teaspoon sugar

2 tablespoons oregano leaves

500 g (1 lb 2 oz) wholemeal
   (whole-wheat) fusilli

Heat the olive oil in a saucepan or frying pan over medium–high heat. Cook the sausages for 6 minutes, turning occasionally. Lift them out onto a plate.

Reduce the heat to medium and cook the onion, capsicum and garlic for 4 minutes. Add the tomatoes, chilli, sugar, oregano and a pinch of sea salt. Simmer for 10 minutes, or until the sauce has thickened.

Slice the sausages, return to the pan and heat through for 2 minutes.

Meanwhile, cook the pasta in a large saucepan of boiling salted water until al dente. Drain well and serve topped with the sauce.

BAKED POLENTA WITH A SIMPLE TOMATO SAUCE

SERVES 4

1 tablespoon sea salt

230 g (8 oz/1¼ cups) instant polenta

1 tablespoon extra virgin olive oil

350 g (12 oz) fresh ricotta

30 g (1 oz/¼ cup) finely grated
  parmesan

TOMATO SAUCE

2 x 400 g (14 oz) tins chopped
  tomatoes

2 tablespoons extra virgin olive oil

1 teaspoon sea salt

1 teaspoon sugar

2 garlic cloves, crushed

Bring 1.5 litres (52 fl oz/6 cups) water to the boil in a large saucepan over high heat. Add the salt and slowly pour in the polenta, stirring constantly with a wooden spoon. Reduce the heat to low, then cover and cook for 10 minutes, stirring regularly.

Lightly oil a 30 x 20 cm (12 x 8 inch) baking dish with half the olive oil. Pour the cooked polenta into the baking dish and spread it out evenly. Leave to cool and firm in the baking dish.

To make the tomato sauce, place the tomatoes in a saucepan over medium heat and cook for 15 minutes, stirring occasionally. Add the olive oil, salt and sugar, season with freshly ground black pepper and cook for 1 minute. Stir in the garlic.

Meanwhile, preheat the oven to 200°C (400°F/Gas 6). Lightly grease a 20 x 25 cm (8 x 10 inch) gratin dish or four individual dishes with the remaining oil.

Turn the polenta out onto a cutting board and cut into 5 cm (2 inch) squares. Place the polenta squares in the greased dish or dishes in a single layer, slightly overlapping them.

Pour the tomato sauce evenly over the polenta. Sprinkle the ricotta and parmesan over the top. Season with black pepper and bake for 30 minutes, or until the cheese is golden.

NOTE

Polenta becomes thick and sticky during cooking. Make sure you stir it regularly so it doesn't catch on the base of the pan.

BAKED MEATBALLS

SERVES 4–6

500 g (1 lb 2 oz) minced (ground)
    beef

1 small onion, grated

55 g (2 oz/⅔ cup firmly packed)
    fresh white breadcrumbs

3 tablespoons chopped flat-leaf
    (Italian) parsley

3 tablespoons chopped coriander
    (cilantro) leaves

1 egg, lightly beaten

1 teaspoon ground cumin

1 teaspoon sweet paprika

2 red chillies, finely chopped

3 tablespoons olive oil

2 x 400 g (14 oz) tins chopped
    tomatoes

½ teaspoon sugar

ROAST CHILLI POTATOES

1 kg (2 lb 4 oz) potatoes, peeled
    and roughly diced

2 tablespoons olive oil

1 long red chilli, thinly sliced

3 spring onions (scallions),
    thinly sliced

2 tablespoons chopped coriander
    (cilantro) leaves

Preheat the oven to 220°C (425°F/Gas 7). To roast the potatoes, toss the potatoes with the olive oil, place on a large baking tray and season with sea salt. Roast for 40 minutes, turning once, until golden and crispy.

Meanwhile, make the meatballs. Combine the meat in a large bowl with the onion, breadcrumbs, parsley, coriander, egg, cumin, paprika and half the chilli. Season with sea salt and freshly ground black pepper and mix gently with your hands. Shape the mixture into small balls (I find wetting my hands makes this easier).

Place the meatballs in a roasting tin. Drizzle with the olive oil and gently toss to coat. Bake in the oven with the potatoes for 10–15 minutes.

Place a frying pan over medium heat. Add the meatballs, tomatoes, sugar, remaining chilli and some more salt and pepper. Stir the meatballs carefully to coat in the sauce, then simmer for 20 minutes.

Scatter the roasted potatoes with the chilli, spring onion and coriander. Return to the oven for a final 2 minutes, before serving with the meatballs.

NOTE

Instead of minced (ground) beef, you can use a mixture of minced pork and veal for the meatballs.

"I find dessert is always an appreciated treat, but it doesn't have to be rich or difficult to make. It can be as simple as vanilla ice cream with fresh berries. Remember, just keep it simple."

POACHED NECTARINES WITH SWEET VANILLA RICOTTA

SERVES 4

4 nectarines
1 litre (35 fl oz/4 cups) cranberry juice
2 tablespoons caster (superfine) sugar
1 cinnamon stick
2 wide strips of lemon rind

SWEET VANILLA RICOTTA

115 g (4 oz/½ cup) fresh ricotta
130 g (4¾ oz/½ cup) creamy yoghurt
1 tablespoon caster (superfine) sugar
1 teaspoon vanilla bean paste

Score a small cross in the base of each nectarine. Place the nectarines in a large bowl and pour in enough boiling water to cover them. Leave for 1 minute, then rinse under cold running water. Peel the skin away from the cross, then cut each nectarine into quarters, removing the stones.

Put the cranberry juice, sugar, cinnamon stick and lemon rind strips in a large saucepan. Stir over medium heat until the sugar dissolves. Bring to the boil, then reduce the heat and simmer for 5 minutes.

Add the nectarines and simmer gently for 5 minutes, or until tender. Remove the nectarines from the poaching liquid with a slotted spoon and set aside to cool.

Bring the poaching liquid back to the boil and simmer until reduced by half. Set aside to cool, then pour over the nectarines and chill until ready to serve.

Stir together the sweet vanilla ricotta ingredients and serve with the nectarines.

STEWED APPLES WITH BLUEBERRIES AND YOGHURT

SERVES 6

8 granny smith apples, peeled,
    cored and cut into eighths

TO SERVE
low-fat yoghurt
blueberries

Put the apples in a saucepan over low heat, with a few tablespoons of water to stop them sticking to the pan. Cover and cook for 20 minutes, stirring occasionally, until the apples are softened but not mushy. Leave to cool.

Serve topped with a good tablespoon of yoghurt and a handful of blueberries.

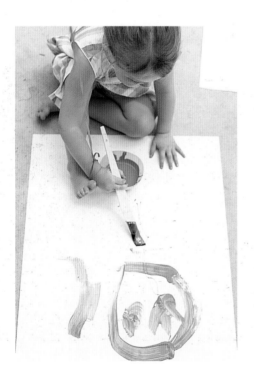

NOTE

Leftover stewed apple will keep for a week in the fridge, and is also great for snacks or on cereal in the morning. It can be blended or mashed for babies.

STRAWBERRIES WITH CHANTILLY CREAM

SERVES 4

500 g (1 lb 2 oz/2 punnets)
   strawberries

250 ml (9 fl oz/1 cup) cream

2 tablespoons caster (superfine)
   sugar

1 teaspoon vanilla extract

TO SERVE

icing (confectioners') sugar,
   for dusting

Hull the strawberries, and cut them in half if large. Whisk together the cream, caster sugar and vanilla extract until soft peaks form. Do not over-whisk.

Pile the strawberries into serving dishes. Sift a little icing sugar over them and top with the chantilly cream.

FRESH PASSIONFRUIT TRIFLE

SERVES 6

300 ml (10½ fl oz) cream

2 tablespoons fresh orange juice, plus about 250 ml (9 fl oz/1 cup) extra, for drizzling (see Note)

2 tablespoons icing (confectioners') sugar

1 teaspoon vanilla extract

600 g (1 lb 5 oz) sponge cake, cut into cubes

PASSIONFRUIT SYRUP

250 g (9 oz/1 cup) passionfruit pulp (from about 12 passionfruit)

110 g (3¾ oz/½ cup) caster (superfine) sugar

To make the passionfruit syrup, put the passionfruit pulp, sugar and 125 ml (4 fl oz/½ cup) water in a saucepan over medium heat. Stir well to dissolve the sugar, then boil for 10 minutes, or until the syrup has a jammy consistency. Leave to cool.

Whisk together the cream, the 2 tablespoons orange juice, the icing sugar and vanilla extract until soft peaks form.

Place half the sponge cubes into six serving dishes. Drizzle with half the extra orange juice, then top with half the cream and half the passionfruit syrup. Repeat the layers and serve.

NOTE

For a grown-ups only dessert, substitute the orange juice with dessert wine.

APPLE AND PASSIONFRUIT CRUMBLE

SERVES 4

6 granny smith apples, peeled
  and thinly sliced
110 g (3¾ oz/½ cup) sugar
pulp from 8 passionfruit

TOPPING
100 g (3½ oz/1 cup) rolled
  (porridge) oats
125 g (4½ oz/⅔ cup lightly packed)
  brown sugar
40 g (1½ oz/⅓ cup) plain
  (all-purpose) flour
100 g (3½ oz) butter, softened

TO SERVE
vanilla ice cream or thick cream

Preheat the oven to 180°C (350°F/Gas 4) and grease a 2 litre (70 fl oz/8 cup) baking dish.

Mix together the apples, sugar and passionfruit pulp, then spread the mixture in the baking dish.

Put the oats, sugar, flour and butter in a bowl and rub together with your hands to make a crumbly topping.

Sprinkle over the fruit and bake for 25–30 minutes, or until the topping is golden. Serve with ice cream or cream.

FAMILY FEASTS

I believe it's really important to develop your children's palates. After all, they are going to be the people you are sharing meals with for the next 20 years, and who wants to dine with fussy eaters? I cook dinner at home every night, so I've got a vested interest in making sure my kids don't request special food and push me into the 'cooking two meals' scenario. Occasionally we'll get them fed early, if we're having friends over for dinner, but Natalie and I are great believers in not giving the girls anything we wouldn't eat ourselves. Special children's menus drive me crazy too — you don't see kids' menus in Chinatown or at Italian restaurants. Grab an extra plate or two and let them explore the food you eat.

STIR-FRIED BEEF WITH NOODLES

SERVES 4–6

250 g (9 oz) fresh egg noodles

3 tablespoons oyster sauce

2 tablespoons soy sauce

1½ tablespoons dry sherry

3 tablespoons chicken stock

2 teaspoons sugar

1 tablespoon light-flavoured oil
  (I like canola)

400 g (14 oz) beef fillet or rump,
  sliced

4 cm (1½ inch) piece of ginger,
  julienned or grated

200 g (7 oz) sugar snap peas

Cook the noodles in boiling water according to the packet instructions. Drain and set aside.

Meanwhile, stir together the oyster sauce, soy sauce, sherry, stock and sugar in a small bowl. Set aside.

Heat a wok or large frying pan over high heat. Add the oil and, when smoking, stir-fry the beef in two batches, cooking for 1 minute, or until it is sealed and browned. Remove from the wok and set aside.

Stir-fry the ginger and peas for 2 minutes, adding a little more oil if needed. Return the beef to the pan and add the oyster sauce mixture. Cook for 1 minute, or until the sauce has thickened slightly.

Add the noodles to the wok and toss well, or divide the noodles among serving bowls and top with the stir-fry.

BARLEY, BEAN AND VEGETABLE SOUP

SERVES 4

100 g (3½ oz/½ cup) pearl barley

2 tablespoons olive oil

1 onion, diced

2 zucchini (courgettes), diced

2 red potatoes, peeled and diced

2 garlic cloves, crushed

1 bunch silverbeet (Swiss chard), about 700 g (1 lb 9 oz), finely shredded

1 litre (35 fl oz/4 cups) chicken or vegetable stock

400 g (14 oz) tin cannellini beans, rinsed

200 g (7 oz) green beans, trimmed and cut into short lengths

80 g (2¾ oz/½ cup) fresh or frozen peas

TO SERVE

grated parmesan

Put the barley in a large saucepan, cover with cold water and bring to the boil. Reduce the heat and simmer for 45 minutes, or until the barley is tender. Rinse under cold running water, drain well and set aside.

Meanwhile, heat the olive oil in a large heavy-based saucepan over medium heat. Add the onion and cook, stirring occasionally, for 5 minutes. Add the zucchini, potato, garlic and silverbeet and cook, stirring occasionally, for another 5 minutes, or until the silverbeet has wilted.

Pour in the stock and 1 litre (35 fl oz/4 cups) water and bring to the boil. Reduce the heat to low and simmer for 20 minutes.

Add the cannellini beans and simmer for another 20 minutes.

Add the barley, beans and peas and simmer for 5–10 minutes, or until the vegetables are tender. Season to taste with sea salt and freshly ground black pepper. Serve sprinkled with parmesan.

PORK CUTLETS WITH APPLE SAUCE AND SWEET AND SOUR CABBAGE

SERVES 4

1 tablespoon olive oil

4 pork loin cutlets

3 granny smith apples, peeled, cored and diced

2 teaspoons caster (superfine) sugar

SWEET AND SOUR CABBAGE

2 tablespoons olive oil

1 small red onion, thinly sliced

1 garlic clove, thinly sliced

1 teaspoon ground cumin

½ red cabbage, shredded

1 tablespoon brown sugar

2 tablespoons balsamic vinegar

To make the sweet and sour cabbage, heat the olive oil in a large saucepan over medium heat. Add the onion, season with sea salt and cook, stirring occasionally, for 5 minutes, or until the onion is soft. Stir in the garlic and cumin and cook for another minute. Add the cabbage and cook for 15 minutes, tossing often. Finally, add the sugar and vinegar and season with freshly ground black pepper. Cook for a final 2 minutes.

Meanwhile, preheat the oven to 180°C (350°F/Gas 4). Heat the olive oil in a large frying pan over high heat. Add the pork and cook for 2 minutes on each side, or until golden. Transfer the cutlets to a baking tray and bake for 5 minutes, or until just cooked through. Cover with foil and leave to rest while making the apple sauce.

While the pork is baking in the oven, return the pan to medium–high heat. Add the apples, 2 tablespoons water and sprinkle with the sugar. Cook, stirring occasionally, for 6–7 minutes, or until the apples are soft.

Serve the cutlets with the apple sauce and cabbage.

CARAMEL CHICKEN

SERVES 4

8 chicken thigh fillets, skinless, chopped in half

1 tablespoon vegetable oil

1 red onion, sliced

3 garlic cloves, sliced

3 tablespoons dark soy sauce

110 g (3¾ oz/½ cup firmly packed) brown sugar

3 tablespoons fish sauce

TO SERVE

steamed rice

steamed green vegetables, such as snow peas (mangetout), asparagus or Chinese broccoli

Place the chicken and vegetable oil in a bowl and toss to combine. Heat a large frying pan over high heat until hot. Cook the chicken in two batches for 2 minutes on one side, or until lightly brown, then turn and cook for another minute. Remove from the pan.

Reduce the heat to medium and add a little extra oil if needed. Add the onion and garlic and cook for 5 minutes, stirring occasionally.

Return the chicken to the pan. Season with freshly ground black pepper, add the soy sauce and stir to combine. Cover the pan, reduce the heat to low and cook for 10 minutes, stirring occasionally.

Increase the heat to high, add the sugar and stir to combine. Cook, uncovered, for 3–4 minutes, or until the sauce is rich, dark and syrupy. Add the fish sauce and stir to combine.

Serve with steamed rice and green vegetables.

CHICKEN, TOMATO AND FENNEL CASSEROLE WITH GARLIC TOASTS

SERVES 4

2 tablespoons olive oil

8 chicken thigh cutlets on the bone, with skin

1 onion, sliced

1 large fennel bulb, trimmed and thinly sliced

2 garlic cloves, crushed

½ teaspoon crushed fennel seeds

2 teaspoons paprika

½ teaspoon saffron threads, soaked in 1 tablespoon water

1 wide orange rind strip

400 g (14 oz) tin chopped tomatoes

500 ml (17 fl oz/2 cups) chicken stock

1 red capsicum (pepper), roasted and thinly sliced

2 teaspoons honey

GARLIC TOASTS

6 garlic cloves, peeled

2 tablespoons olive oil

2 tablespoons butter

1 tablespoon chopped flat-leaf (Italian) parsley

8 slices baguette

Heat the olive oil in a large heavy-based saucepan over medium-high heat. Add the chicken (in batches, if necessary) and brown for 2–3 minutes on each side. Remove from the pan and set aside. Drain most of the oil from the pan, leaving only about 1 tablespoon.

Reduce the heat to medium and add the onion and fennel to the pan. Cook, stirring occasionally, for 7–8 minutes, or until the vegetables are soft. Add the garlic, fennel seeds and paprika and cook, stirring, for another minute. Add the saffron with its liquid, the orange rind, tomatoes, stock and capsicum and stir well.

Return the chicken to the pan, bring to the boil, then reduce the heat to low. Cover and simmer for 30 minutes, or until the chicken is cooked through and tender. Skim any oil from the top of the casserole. Stir in the honey, then season to taste with sea salt and freshly ground black pepper.

Meanwhile, preheat the oven to 180°C (350°F/Gas 4). To make the garlic toasts, put the garlic and olive oil in a small roasting tin and season with salt and pepper. Cover with foil and roast for 20 minutes. Remove from the oven and leave to cool slightly, then mash the garlic in a bowl with a fork. Add the butter and parsley and mash together. Arrange the bread slices on a baking tray, spread with the garlic butter and bake for 5–10 minutes, or until the toasts are crisp.

Serve the casserole with the hot garlic toasts.

TAGLIATELLE WITH CHICKEN AND GREEN BEANS

SERVES 4

2 x 200 g (7 oz) skinless chicken breasts, thinly sliced

2 tablespoons extra virgin olive oil

3 garlic cloves, finely sliced

375 g (13 oz) tagliatelle

2 tablespoons olive oil

200 g (7 oz) baby green beans, topped but not tailed, sliced from end to end on the diagonal

125 ml (4 fl oz/½ cup) chicken stock

TO SERVE
grated parmesan

basil leaves

Place the chicken, extra virgin olive oil and garlic in a bowl and stir to combine. Season with sea salt and freshly ground black pepper. Set aside to marinate briefly.

Cook the pasta in a large pot of rapidly boiling salted water until al dente. Drain well.

Meanwhile, about 5 minutes before the pasta is cooked, place a large frying pan over high heat until hot. Add the olive oil and heat for 5 seconds. Add the chicken with the marinade and sear quickly for 30 seconds.

Add the beans, reduce the heat to medium and cook for another 2 minutes, stirring occasionally. Return the heat to high, add the stock and simmer for 30 seconds.

Add the pasta and toss to combine. Divide the pasta among serving bowls. Serve topped with parmesan, basil and freshly ground black pepper.

NOTE
You can use any type of tagliatelle for this dish – spinach tagliatelle goes especially well.

SWEET POTATO AND CHICKPEA TAGINE

SERVES 4

2 tablespoons olive oil

1 large onion, finely chopped

2 garlic cloves, crushed

2 teaspoons grated fresh ginger

2 teaspoons ground cumin

1 cinnamon stick

400 ml (14 fl oz) vegetable stock

½ teaspoon saffron threads, soaked
  in 3 tablespoons cold water

800 g (1 lb 12 oz) sweet potatoes,
  peeled and cut into small cubes

400 g (14 oz) tin chickpeas, rinsed

200 g (7 oz) green beans, trimmed
  and cut into short lengths

1 teaspoon honey

TO SERVE

steamed couscous

plain yoghurt

chopped coriander (cilantro)

Heat the olive oil in a large heavy-based saucepan over medium heat. Add the onion and cook, stirring occasionally, for 5–6 minutes, or until the onion is soft. Add the garlic, ginger, cumin and cinnamon and cook, stirring, for 1–2 minutes, or until fragrant.

Add the stock and the saffron threads in their water. Bring to the boil. Add the sweet potato, reduce the heat, then cover and simmer for 15 minutes, or until the sweet potato is tender.

Add the chickpeas and beans and simmer for 5 minutes, or until the beans are bright green and tender. Stir the honey through and season to taste with sea salt and freshly ground black pepper.

Serve the tagine on a bed of couscous, topped with some yoghurt and chopped coriander.

MINUTE STEAK WITH GREEN BEANS AND TOMATOES

SERVES 4

2 tablespoons olive oil, plus extra
    for brushing

3 garlic cloves, thinly sliced

1 small red chilli, chopped, or
    ¼ teaspoon chilli flakes

500 g (1 lb 2 oz) tomatoes, chopped

500 g (1 lb 2 oz) green beans,
    trimmed

4 minute steaks, about 100 g
    (3½ oz) each

TO SERVE

lemon wedges

chopped flat-leaf (Italian) parsley

Heat a saucepan over medium–high heat. Add the olive oil, garlic, chilli and a good sprinkling of sea salt. Cook, stirring, for 30 seconds, or until the garlic is golden. Add the tomatoes, reduce the heat to medium and cook for 10 minutes, stirring occasionally.

Meanwhile, place a large saucepan of water over high heat and bring to the boil. Add the beans and cook for 4 minutes. Drain, then add to the tomatoes with some freshly ground black pepper. Toss well and cook for a few minutes longer.

Just before serving, heat a frying pan over high heat. Brush the steaks with olive oil and sprinkle with salt and pepper. Cook for 1 minute on each side, or until cooked to your liking.

Serve the steaks with lemon wedges and the green beans and tomatoes, sprinkled with parsley.

SUNDAY ROAST CHICKEN WITH CORIANDER CHILLI STUFFING AND COCONUT GRAVY

SERVES 4

1.6 kg (3 lb 8 oz) free-range chicken

2 tablespoons olive oil

CORIANDER CHILLI STUFFING

3 large handfuls coriander (cilantro) leaves and stems

45 g (1½ oz/½ cup) desiccated coconut

4 long green chillies, seeded and roughly chopped

4 garlic cloves, chopped

2 teaspoons grated fresh ginger

juice of 2 limes

2 teaspoons brown sugar

COCONUT GRAVY

1 tablespoon green curry paste

250 ml (9 fl oz/1 cup) light coconut milk

1 tablespoon lime juice

2 teaspoons fish sauce

1 teaspoon brown sugar

TO SERVE

roast potatoes

steamed Asian greens

Preheat the oven to 220°C (425°F/Gas 7).

To make the stuffing, mix the coriander, coconut, chilli, garlic and ginger in a food processor until finely chopped. Stir in the lime juice and sugar and season to taste with sea salt and freshly ground black pepper.

Rinse the chicken and pat dry. With your fingers, carefully loosen the skin over the breast of the chicken and down to the thigh area. Push half the stuffing under the skin, spreading it to cover the breast and thigh. Put the remaining stuffing inside the cavity of the chicken. Tie the legs together with kitchen string.

Put the chicken, breast side up, in a large roasting tin. Drizzle with the olive oil and season with salt and pepper. Roast for 20 minutes, then reduce the oven temperature to 200°C (400°F/Gas 6). Roast for another 50 minutes, or until the juices run clear when you prick the thickest part of the thigh (cover the chicken with foil if it's browning too quickly). Let the chicken rest for 10 minutes before carving.

While the chicken is resting, make the coconut gravy. Heat a small saucepan over medium heat. Add the curry paste and cook, stirring, for 2 minutes, or until fragrant. Stir in the coconut milk and simmer for 2–3 minutes. Stir in the lime juice, fish sauce and sugar.

Serve the chicken with the coconut gravy, roast potatoes and steamed greens.

LAMB KOFTAS WITH BOMBAY POTATO SALAD

SERVES 4

500 g (1 lb 2 oz) minced (ground) lamb

1 teaspoon sea salt

1 teaspoon ground cumin

1 teaspoon ground coriander

2–3 tablespoons chopped coriander (cilantro) leaves

2 white onions, grated

1 small green chilli, finely chopped

2 tablespoons olive oil

BOMBAY POTATO SALAD

750 g (1 lb 10 oz) waxy potatoes, such as kipfler (fingerling), peeled and diagonally sliced

1½ teaspoons sea salt

4 tablespoons extra virgin olive oil

3 tablespoons lime juice

2 teaspoons yellow mustard seeds, briefly dry-fried until fragrant

2 teaspoons ground turmeric

1 small green capsicum (pepper), finely diced

2–3 tablespoons coriander (cilantro) leaves

6 spring onions (scallions), sliced

TO SERVE

lime wedges

mango chutney

tomato salsa

To make the potato salad, bring a large saucepan of water to the boil over high heat. Add the potatoes and 1 teaspoon of the salt, then reduce the heat to medium and simmer for 8–10 minutes, or until the potatoes are tender when pierced with a knife. Undercook the potatoes a little because they will continue cooking when removed from the water.

Stir together the olive oil, lime juice, mustard seeds and turmeric; season with freshly ground black pepper and the remaining salt. Pour half the dressing over the hot potatoes and stir gently. Leave to cool, then add the capsicum, coriander, spring onion and remaining dressing and stir gently.

To make the koftas, put the lamb, salt, cumin, ground coriander, fresh coriander, onion and chilli in a bowl. Season with pepper and mix together. Shape tablespoons of the mixture into balls and thread onto skewers.

Heat a barbecue or large frying pan over medium–high heat and add the olive oil. Cook the koftas in batches until browned.

Serve the koftas with the potato salad, with lime wedges, mango chutney and tomato salsa on the side.

CHICKEN BURGERS WITH LEMONGRASS AND LIME

SERVES 6

600 g (1 lb 5 oz) minced (ground) chicken

1 onion, finely grated

85 g (3 oz/1 cup firmly packed) fresh white breadcrumbs

1 garlic clove, crushed

1 lemongrass stem, white part only, finely chopped

2 tablespoons chopped coriander (cilantro)

2 teaspoons finely grated lime zest

1 tablespoon fish sauce

2 teaspoons caster (superfine) sugar

light-flavoured oil (such as grapeseed or canola), for brushing

TO SERVE

6 soft bread rolls

lettuce leaves

mint leaves

coriander (cilantro) leaves

chilli sauce

Put the chicken, onion, breadcrumbs, garlic, lemongrass, coriander, lime zest, fish sauce and sugar in a large bowl and mix together well with your hands. Shape into six patties, then cover and refrigerate for 30 minutes.

Heat a barbecue or chargrill pan and brush with a little oil. Cook the patties for 4 minutes on each side, or until cooked through.

Serve on soft rolls with some lettuce, mint and coriander leaves and chilli sauce.

FISH BURRITOS

SERVES 4

1 cup roughly chopped coriander
   (cilantro) leaves and stems

2 teaspoons paprika

1 teaspoon cumin

1 teaspoon sea salt

1 small red chilli, seeded and
   chopped

grated zest of 1 lime

80 ml (2½ fl oz/⅓ cup) olive oil

750 g (1 lb 10 oz) snapper fillets,
   or other firm white fish, skin and
   any small bones removed, flesh
   cut into strips

CUCUMBER SALAD

1 telegraph (long) cucumber

250 g (9 oz/1 punnet) cherry
   tomatoes, sliced in half

4 spring onions (scallions), sliced

3 tablespoons coriander (cilantro)
   leaves

1 teaspoon lime juice

1 small red chilli, seeded and finely
   sliced

1 teaspoon sea salt

1 teaspoon caster (superfine) sugar

TO SERVE

baby cos (romaine) lettuce leaves

8 fresh tortillas, warmed (see Note)

lime cheeks

Place the coriander, spices, chilli, lime zest and olive oil in a blender or a food processor. Season with freshly ground black pepper and process until a paste forms.

Place the fish in a bowl, add the spice paste and gently stir to combine. Leave to marinate for 15 minutes.

Meanwhile, make the cucumber salad. Peel the cucumber and slice in half lengthways, then remove the seeds with a teaspoon. Thinly slice the flesh, then place in a bowl with the remaining salad ingredients. Gently toss to combine.

Heat a non-stick frying pan over high heat until hot. Add some of the fish strips in a single layer and cook for 2 minutes. Turn and cook on the other side for 1 minute, or until the fish is opaque and just cooked. Remove from the pan and cook the remaining fish.

To serve, place some lettuce leaves on each warm tortilla, then top with the fish strips and cucumber salad. Fold in half and serve with lime cheeks.

NOTE

To warm the tortillas, wrap them in foil and place in a 200°C (400°F/Gas 6) oven for 5 minutes.

SPAGHETTI WITH CHERRY TOMATOES, RICOTTA, SPINACH AND PECORINO

SERVES 4

750 g (1 lb 10 oz) cherry tomatoes

4 garlic cloves, sliced

1 red onion, thinly sliced

1 tablespoon oregano leaves

100 ml (3½ fl oz) extra virgin olive oil

500 g (1 lb 2 oz) fresh spaghetti

45 g (1½ oz/1 cup) baby English spinach leaves

200 g (7 oz) fresh ricotta

80 g (2¾ oz/¾ cup) grated pecorino cheese

Preheat the oven to 180°C (350°F/Gas 4).

Put the tomatoes, garlic, onion and oregano on a baking tray and drizzle with the olive oil. Roast for 20–25 minutes, or until the tomatoes have wilted.

Cook the pasta in a large saucepan of boiling salted water until al dente. Drain and toss with the tomato mixture, spinach and half the ricotta.

Divide among serving bowls, top with the remaining ricotta and season to taste with freshly ground black pepper. Serve sprinkled with the pecorino.

PARMESAN-CRUSTED BLUE-EYE AND BRAISED POTATOES WITH PEAS

SERVES 4

80 g (2¾ oz/1 cup firmly packed) fresh breadcrumbs

50 g (1¾ oz oz/½ cup) finely grated parmesan

2 eggs

125 g (4½ oz/1 cup) plain (all-purpose) flour

4 blue-eye or other firm white fish fillets

1 tablespoon olive oil

25 g (1 oz) butter

BRAISED POTATOES WITH PEAS

8 kipfler (fingerling) potatoes

1 tablespoon olive oil

1 white onion, finely sliced into rings

155 g (5½ oz/1 cup) green peas

250 ml (9 fl oz/1 cup) chicken stock

15 g (½ oz) butter

TO SERVE

mint leaves

Mix the breadcrumbs and parmesan in a bowl and season with sea salt and freshly ground black pepper. Crack the eggs into a second bowl and lightly beat together. Place the flour and some salt and pepper in a third bowl.

Dip a fish fillet in the flour, then in the egg, and finally in the breadcrumb mixture. Continue until all the fish is coated. (This can be done in advance if you wish. Cover and refrigerate for up to 2 hours before cooking.)

Next, prepare the braised potatoes. Scrub the potatoes but leave the skins on. Bring a saucepan of water to the boil and place the potatoes in a steamer basket on top of the saucepan. Cover and gently steam for 10–15 minutes, or until tender. Remove and allow to cool slightly, then slice the potatoes into discs.

Heat the olive oil in a saucepan over medium heat and fry the onion until soft, but not brown. Add the peas and toss well. Add the stock, bring to the boil and simmer for 5 minutes. Add the potatoes and cook for another 2 minutes. Remove the pan from the heat, add the butter, season with salt and pepper and stir to combine. Keep warm while cooking the fish.

Heat the olive oil and butter in a large non-stick frying pan over medium–high heat. Add the fish and cook for about 2 minutes on each side, turning once, until lightly golden. (Cook the fish in two batches if your pan is a bit too small.)

Divide the fish and potatoes among four shallow bowls. Sprinkle mint leaves over the potatoes and serve.

VEAL CUTLETS WITH TOMATOES, CAPERS AND POLENTA

SERVES 4

4 large ripe tomatoes, each cut
    into 8 wedges

1 tablespoon oregano leaves

2 tablespoons capers, rinsed and
    squeezed dry

2 garlic cloves, sliced

1 red onion, cut into fine wedges

2 tablespoons olive oil, plus extra
    for brushing

4 veal cutlets

POLENTA

1 tablespoon sea salt

250 g (9 oz/1⅓ cups) polenta

45 g (1½ oz/½ cup) finely grated
    parmesan

To make the polenta, you'll need a large heatproof bowl that will sit over a large saucepan. Fill the saucepan two-thirds with water, but make sure the base of the bowl will not touch the water. Bring the water to the boil. Pour another 1.75 litres (61 fl oz/7 cups) boiling water into the heatproof bowl, add the salt and polenta and whisk continuously for about 4 minutes, until the mixture thickens. Cover the bowl tightly with foil and sit the bowl over the saucepan of steadily boiling water. After 20 minutes, remove the bowl, carefully lift off the foil and thoroughly stir the polenta.

Cover the bowl again and return to the heat. Keep stirring the polenta every 20 minutes. It should be ready after it has cooked for about 1½ hours.

About an hour before serving time, preheat the oven to 200°C (400°F/Gas 6). Put the tomatoes, oregano, capers, garlic, onion and olive oil in a small roasting tin (large enough to fit the veal cutlets) and toss together. Sprinkle with sea salt and freshly ground black pepper. Cover with foil and bake for 25–30 minutes. Remove the foil and bake for another 10 minutes.

While the tomatoes are roasting, brush the veal cutlets with oil and season liberally with salt and pepper. Heat a large frying pan over high heat for 1–2 minutes, until very hot. Add the cutlets and cook for 1 minute on each side, or until the meat is sealed. Remove from the pan.

Place the cutlets on top of the tomatoes and bake for another 10–15 minutes, or until the veal is cooked.

Stir the parmesan through the polenta and serve with the cutlets and roasted tomatoes.

GIOVANNI'S SAUSAGES WITH ROSEMARY ROASTED POTATOES

SERVES 4

6 Italian-style sausages

800 g (1 lb 12 oz) potatoes, scrubbed and sliced (I use kipfler/fingerling potatoes)

1½ teaspoons paprika

2 rosemary sprigs

½ ciabatta loaf, crust removed

50 ml (1¾ fl oz) extra virgin olive oil

SHREDDED RADICCHIO SALAD

2 radicchio, shredded

4 tablespoons extra virgin olive oil

1½ tablespoons orange juice

a pinch of sugar

TO SERVE

basil leaves

rocket (arugula) leaves

Preheat the oven to 200°C (400°F/Gas 6).

Slice the sausages thickly and place in a large roasting tin. Add the potatoes, paprika and rosemary and season with sea salt and freshly ground black pepper. Tear the ciabatta into bite-sized pieces and add to the roasting tin. Drizzle with the olive oil and toss gently.

Transfer to the oven and roast, stirring occasionally, for 30–40 minutes, or until the potatoes are tender and the sausages and bread are golden brown.

Meanwhile, make the salad. Put the radicchio in a bowl. Mix together the olive oil, orange juice and sugar and toss with the radicchio.

Sprinkle the potatoes and sausages with basil and serve with rocket leaves and the radicchio salad.

CHICKEN SCHNITZEL WITH FENNEL SLAW

SERVES 4

4 chicken breasts, skin removed

60 g (2¼ oz/½ cup) plain (all-purpose) flour

1 egg

2 tablespoons milk

160 g (5¾ oz/2 cups firmly packed) fresh breadcrumbs

3 tablespoons chopped flat-leaf (Italian) parsley

3 tablespoons chopped chervil

3 tablespoons chopped oregano

20 g (¾ oz) butter

125 ml (4 fl oz/½ cup) olive oil

FENNEL SLAW

3 fennel bulbs, finely sliced

2 tablespoons small salted capers, rinsed

1 small red onion, finely sliced

1½ tablespoons chopped flat-leaf (Italian) parsley

3 tablespoons whole-egg mayonnaise

1½ tablespoons lemon juice

MASH

800 g (1 lb 12 oz) mashing potatoes, peeled and chopped

185 ml (6 fl oz/¾ cup) milk or cream

80 g (2¾ oz) butter

Lay each chicken breast between two sheets of plastic wrap and flatten slightly with a meat mallet or rolling pin. Cut each flattened breast in half.

Put the flour in a shallow bowl and season with plenty of sea salt and freshly ground black pepper. In a second bowl, lightly beat the egg and milk together. Mix the breadcrumbs and herbs in a third bowl and season with salt and pepper.

Dip each chicken fillet in flour to coat, then in the egg mixture and lastly in the breadcrumbs. (This can be done in advance if you wish. Cover and refrigerate for up to 2 hours before cooking.)

To make the fennel slaw, put the fennel, capers, onion and parsley in a bowl. Mix together the mayonnaise and lemon juice and stir through the slaw. Season with salt and pepper.

To make the mash, boil the potatoes until tender. Drain, return to the hot pan and mash. Beat in the milk, butter and a pinch of salt, until the mash is smooth and creamy. Keep warm.

Meanwhile, heat the butter and olive oil in a large non-stick frying pan over medium heat. Cook the schnitzels for 3 minutes on each side, or until golden brown and cooked through (don't overcrowd the pan: cook them in batches if necessary). Drain on kitchen paper and keep warm until all the chicken is cooked.

Serve the schnitzels on a bed of mash, with the fennel slaw on the side.

BANANA BUTTERSCOTCH PUDDING

SERVES 4

125 g (4½ oz/1 cup) plain
  (all-purpose) flour

a pinch of salt

110 g (3¾ oz/½ cup) caster
  (superfine) sugar

3 teaspoons baking powder

1 banana, mashed

250 ml (9 fl oz/1 cup) milk

85 g (3 oz) unsalted butter, melted

1 egg, lightly beaten

1 teaspoon vanilla extract

TOPPING

150 g (5½ oz/¾ cup lightly packed)
  brown sugar

3 tablespoons golden syrup

TO SERVE

vanilla ice cream or thick cream

Preheat the oven to 180°C (350°F/Gas 4). Grease a
2 litre (70 fl oz/8 cup) baking dish.

Sift the flour, salt, sugar and baking powder into a bowl.
Add the banana, milk, butter, egg and vanilla extract and
whisk together well. Pour into the baking dish and place
the dish on a baking tray.

To make the topping, put the sugar, golden syrup and
250 ml (9 fl oz/1 cup) boiling water in a small saucepan
and bring to the boil.

Carefully pour the topping over the pudding, then bake
for 30–40 minutes, or until the pudding is cooked
through. Serve with ice cream or cream.

VANILLA RICE PUDDING WITH RHUBARB

SERVES 4

1 litre (35 fl oz/4 cups) milk

75 g (2¾ oz/⅓ cup) sugar

2 orange rind strips

1 vanilla bean, seeds scraped,
   or 1 teaspoon vanilla extract

180 g (6½ oz) arborio rice

3 egg yolks

BAKED RHUBARB

500 g (1 lb 2 oz/1 bunch) rhubarb

110 g (3¾ oz/½ cup) caster
   (superfine) sugar

Start by baking the rhubarb. Preheat the oven to 180°C (350°F/Gas 4). Trim the base and leaves from the rhubarb. Rinse the stems and cut them into short lengths, then toss thoroughly with the sugar. Place in a stainless steel, non-stick or ceramic baking dish, making sure the rhubarb is covered with sugar. Cover tightly with foil and bake for 35–45 minutes, or until soft. Let the rhubarb cool in the syrup that has formed.

Meanwhile, put the milk, sugar and orange rind strips in a saucepan with the vanilla bean and seeds. Bring to a simmer over medium heat. Stir in the rice and cook for 30 minutes, or until the rice is tender, stirring occasionally to stop it sticking to the bottom of the pan.

Add the egg yolks to the rice one at a time, mixing well. Remove from the heat and stand for 5 minutes. Remove the orange rind strips and vanilla bean.

Spoon the rice pudding into serving bowls. Top with the baked rhubarb and the rhubarb syrup.

BREAD AND BUTTER PUDDING

SERVES 6

175 g (6 oz/½ cup) golden syrup

1 loaf wholemeal (whole-wheat)
   bread

40 g (1½ oz) butter, softened

60 g (2¼ oz/⅓ cup) sultanas
   (golden raisins)

2 eggs, plus 6 egg yolks

500 ml (17 fl oz/2 cups) milk

375 ml (13 fl oz/1½ cups) cream

2 teaspoons vanilla extract

110 g (3¾ oz/½ cup) caster
   (superfine) sugar, plus 1 tablespoon
   for sprinkling

1 tablespoon grated orange zest

TO SERVE

cream

Lightly grease a 2.5 litre (87 fl oz/10 cup) baking dish and swirl the golden syrup over the base and side of the dish. Butter the bread, cut each slice in half and arrange one layer in the bottom of the dish. Sprinkle with some sultanas and top with another layer of bread. Repeat the layers until you've used all the bread and sultanas.

In a bowl, whisk together the eggs, extra yolks, milk, cream, vanilla extract, sugar and orange zest. Carefully pour the mixture over the bread and leave for 30 minutes. Every 10 minutes or so, press the bread down so that it soaks up all the liquid. Sprinkle with the extra sugar.

Meanwhile, preheat the oven to 180°C (350°F/Gas 4).

Bake the pudding for 50–55 minutes, or until golden brown. Leave the pudding out of the oven for 15 minutes to cool a little, before serving with cream.

PEACH MELBA

SERVES 4

4 peaches
440 g (15½ oz/2 cups) caster
  (superfine) sugar
150 g (4½ oz/1 punnet) raspberries
1 tablespoon lemon juice

TO SERVE
vanilla ice cream

Score a cross into the base of each peach. Put the sugar and 1 litre (35 fl oz/4 cups) water in a saucepan and bring to the boil over high heat. Reduce the heat to low and add the peaches. Simmer for 5–10 minutes, or until the fruit is cooked (I prefer the peaches slightly firm). Remove the peaches from the syrup, allow to cool, then peel.

Increase the heat to high and reduce the syrup by half. Put the raspberries in a blender with the lemon juice and 4 tablespoons of the syrup and blend until smooth.

Place a peach in each serving bowl and drizzle with the raspberry syrup. Serve with a scoop of ice cream.

NOTE

Peaches are available as clingstone or slipstone (freestone) types, the latter arriving later in the season. You can remove the stone more cleanly from slipstone peaches, so they lend themselves much better to recipes that call for sliced peaches.

CARAMEL PECAN SUNDAE

SERVES 6

185 g (6½ oz/1 cup lightly packed)
   brown sugar

250 ml (9 fl oz/1 cup) cream

1 teaspoon vanilla extract

20 g (¾ oz) unsalted butter

TO SERVE

vanilla ice cream

toasted pecans, roughly chopped

Put the sugar, cream, vanilla extract and butter in a small saucepan over medium heat. Stir well and bring to a gentle boil. Cook, stirring occasionally, for 10 minutes, or until the caramel is thick and syrupy. Remove from the heat and leave to cool a little.

Scoop some ice cream into bowls. Drizzle some caramel sauce over the top, sprinkle with pecans and serve.

"Most of us love the indulgence of dessert. As a cook, nothing gives me more satisfaction than making sweet things for people to enjoy."

PARTY TIME

Sweet things have a bad reputation, but I'm a great fan of moderation — there's nothing wrong with the occasional bit of butter and sugar. Still, it's fortunate for all parents that we don't have kids' parties every day!

As the father of three young girls, I want them to have a really healthy attitude to food. Enjoying an occasional chocolate bar or an ice cream after school is fine if they're having a healthy dinner every night. I want my family to grow up with good memories around food; a slice of cake still warm from the oven or a tart made from freshly picked apricots will become part of a young person's happy memory. And when it comes to happy memories, nothing is quite so special as homemade, freshly baked party treats!

CARAMEL POPCORN

MAKES ABOUT 10 CUPFULS

80 g (2¾ oz/⅓ cup) popping corn

200 ml (7 fl oz) sweetened
   condensed milk

110 g (3¾ oz/½ cup firmly packed)
   brown sugar

110 g (3¾ oz/½ cup) caster
   (superfine) sugar

80 g (2¾ oz) unsalted butter

Pop the corn in a pan or in the microwave, following the instructions on the packet.

Preheat the oven to 170°C (325°F/Gas 3). Put the popcorn in a large heatproof bowl and line two large baking trays with baking paper.

Put the condensed milk, brown sugar, caster sugar and butter in a saucepan over low heat and stir until the sugar has dissolved. Bring to the boil, reduce the heat and simmer for 1 minute, or until a caramel forms. Pour over the popcorn and stir with a wooden spoon until all the popcorn is completely covered with the caramel.

Spread the popcorn on the baking trays. Place in the oven and bake for 10–12 minutes, or until the popcorn is golden brown, stirring it occasionally to break up the clumps. Cool completely on the trays before serving.

COCONUT MARSHMALLOWS

MAKES ABOUT 40 PIECES

500 g (1 lb 2 oz) caster (superfine)
   sugar

1 tablespoon glucose syrup

30 g (1 oz) powdered gelatine

2 egg whites

1 teaspoon vanilla extract

icing (confectioners') sugar,
   for dusting

toasted shredded coconut,
   for coating

Put the sugar, glucose syrup and 210 ml (7½ fl oz) water in a large saucepan. Stir over low heat until the sugar has dissolved. Bring to the boil and boil until the syrup reaches 142°C (275°F) on a sugar thermometer; this is called the 'soft crack' stage (see Note). Brush down the side of the pan with a wet pastry brush if any sugar crystals form.

Meanwhile, put 140 ml (4½ fl oz) water in a small heatproof bowl and sprinkle with the gelatine. Place the bowl over a small saucepan of boiling water until the gelatine has dissolved. Add the gelatine to the cooked sugar syrup — take care as the mixture will initially bubble vigorously.

While the gelatine is dissolving, beat the egg whites with electric beaters until stiff peaks form. With the beaters running, gradually add the boiling sugar syrup to the egg whites in a thin stream. Continue beating for 7–8 minutes, or until the mixture becomes thick and holds its shape. Add the vanilla extract and beat until well combined.

Lightly oil a 20 x 30 cm (8 x 12 inch) baking tin and dust with icing sugar. Spread the marshmallow mixture evenly into the tin and smooth the top. Sprinkle with the coconut, pressing it gently into the marshmallow to make it adhere.

Leave overnight, or until set. Turn out of the tin and cut into squares with a hot, wet knife.

NOTE

If you don't have a sugar thermometer, you can test the syrup by dropping a small teaspoonful into a bowl of iced water: the syrup has reached the 'soft crack' stage when you are able to lift out the ball of syrup and stretch it between your fingers into pliable strands.

JAM BUTTONS

MAKES 25–30

250 g (9 oz) unsalted butter, softened

3 tablespoons caster (superfine) sugar

grated zest of 1 orange

1 egg yolk

1 teaspoon vanilla extract

250 g (9 oz/2 cups) plain (all-purpose) flour, sifted

90 g (3¼ oz/1 cup) desiccated coconut

1½ tablespoons raspberry or apricot jam

Preheat the oven to 180°C (350°F/Gas 4) and line a large tray with baking paper.

Beat the butter, sugar and orange zest with electric beaters until pale. Add the egg yolk and vanilla extract and beat until combined. Fold in the flour and coconut.

Roll tablespoons of the dough into balls. Arrange on the baking tray about 2.5 cm (1 inch) apart and press to flatten slightly. Make an indent in the centre of each biscuit with your thumb, then place ½ teaspoon jam in each indent.

Bake for 10–12 minutes, or until lightly browned. Leave to cool on a wire rack.

"Children can really be involved with making these biscuits. There's a lot of rolling, pressing and spooning jam that doesn't need much precision and is great for small helping hands."

MINI CARAMEL TARTS

MAKES 24

250 g (9 oz/2 cups) plain
  (all-purpose) flour
110 g (3¾ oz/½ cup) caster
  (superfine) sugar
115 g (4 oz) unsalted butter
1 egg
chocolate melts (buttons),
  to decorate

FILLING
450 g (1 lb) caster (superfine) sugar
185 ml (6 fl oz/¾ cup) cream
40 g (1½ oz) unsalted butter

Mix the flour, sugar and butter in a food processor until fine crumbs form. Add the egg and pulse until just combined. Turn out onto a clean work surface and lightly knead together. Wrap the dough in plastic wrap and chill for 20 minutes.

Roll out the dough to about 4 mm (¼ inch) thick and use a cutter to cut out 6 cm (2½ inch) rounds. Use the pastry to line two 12-hole patty pans or mini muffin tins and place in the freezer for 15–20 minutes.

Meanwhile, preheat the oven to 200°C (400°F/Gas 6). Bake the tart shells for 15 minutes, or until just golden.

To make the filling, put the sugar in a saucepan with 250 ml (9 fl oz/1 cup) water and boil over high heat for 15 minutes, or until deeply golden. Remove from the heat, then carefully stir in the cream and the butter. Pour into the tart shells and chill for 2 hours.

Decorate the tarts with chocolate buttons and keep in the fridge until ready to serve.

BERRY BUTTERFLY CAKES

MAKES 12

185 g (6½ oz/1½ cups) plain (all-purpose) flour

3 teaspoons baking powder

125 g (4½ oz) unsalted butter, softened

1 teaspoon vanilla extract

150 g (5½ oz/⅔ cup) caster (superfine) sugar

2 eggs

125 ml (4 fl oz/½ cup) milk

TO SERVE

whipped cream

raspberries

sliced strawberries

icing (confectioners') sugar

Preheat the oven to 180°C (350°F/Gas 4). Line a 12-hole muffin tin with large paper cases.

Sift the flour and baking powder into a bowl. Add the butter, vanilla extract, sugar, eggs and milk and mix until smooth, either with electric beaters or a wooden spoon.

Spoon the mixture into the paper cases. Bake for 17–20 minutes, or until golden brown. Leave in the tin for 5 minutes before turning out onto a wire rack to cool.

Slice the tops off the cooled cupcakes, then cut each top in half. Spoon some whipped cream onto the cakes and decorate with raspberries and strawberries. Place the tops back on and sprinkle with icing sugar.

"While electric beaters are great time-savers, I always try to whip cream by hand. It gives me a little more control over the cream and prevents over-beating."

SAUSAGE ROLLS WITH HOMEMADE KETCHUP

MAKES 24

4 sheets frozen puff pastry, thawed

10 thick sausages (about 1 kg/
   2 lb 4 oz)

2 egg yolks

2 tablespoons milk

sesame seeds, for sprinkling

KETCHUP

500 ml (17 fl oz/2 cups) tomato
   passata (puréed tomatoes)

3 tablespoons brown sugar

2 teaspoons worcestershire sauce

1 tablespoon red wine vinegar

Put the ketchup ingredients in a small saucepan over medium heat. Stir well to dissolve the sugar, then simmer for 10 minutes, or until the sauce has thickened.

Preheat the oven to 200°C (400°F/Gas 6). Grease a large baking tray.

Cut the pastry sheets in half. Squeeze the sausage meat out of the casings, down along one long side of each pastry sheet. Mix the egg yolks with the milk and brush along the outside pastry edges. Roll each one up and cut each roll into three pieces. Place on the baking tray, with the sealed edges underneath.

Brush with more egg yolk and sprinkle with sesame seeds. Bake for 20–25 minutes, or until the pastry is golden. Serve with the ketchup.

PARTY PIZZA

MAKES 1

1 pitta bread (I like wholemeal/
  whole-wheat)

125 ml (4 fl oz/½ cup) tomato pasta
  sauce

1 zucchini (courgette) or 1 large field
  mushroom, sliced

70 g (2½ oz) mozzarella cheese,
  sliced

1 tablespoon grated parmesan

1 tablespoon oregano leaves

1 tablespoon extra virgin olive oil

Preheat the oven to 240°C (475°F/Gas 8) and put
a baking tray in the oven to heat up.

Lay the bread on a sheet of baking paper. Spread the
bread with the tomato sauce and top with the zucchini
or mushrooms, then the mozzarella. Sprinkle with the
parmesan and oregano, drizzle with the olive oil and
season with sea salt and freshly ground black pepper.

Remove the hot baking tray from the oven and transfer
the pizza, still on its sheet of baking paper, to the tray.
Return to the oven and bake for 10 minutes, or until
the bread is crisp and the cheese has melted.

CHOCOLATE CAKE

SERVES 10–12

280 g (10 oz/2¼ cups) plain
   (all-purpose) flour

2½ teaspoons baking powder

55 g (2 oz/½ cup) cocoa powder

220 g (7¾ oz/1 cup) caster
   (superfine) sugar

250 g (9 oz) very soft unsalted butter

4 eggs

170 ml (5½ fl oz/⅔ cup) milk

ICING

300 g (10½ oz) dark chocolate,
   broken into pieces

370 g (13 oz/1½ cups) sour cream

TO DECORATE

bright sweets (candy)

candles

Preheat the oven to 180°C (350°F/Gas 4). Grease two 20 cm (8 inch) round cake tins and line with baking paper.

Sift the flour, baking powder, cocoa and sugar into a large bowl and stir together. Add the butter, eggs and milk. Mix with electric beaters on low speed for 1–2 minutes, or until smooth.

Spoon the mixture into the cake tins and bake for 25 minutes, or until a skewer inserted into the centre of the cakes comes out clean. Leave in the tins for 5 minutes before turning out onto wire racks to cool.

To make the icing, put the chocolate in a heatproof bowl over a saucepan of barely simmering water. Heat the chocolate very slowly until just melted, being careful not to let the water boil or touch the bottom of the bowl. Remove from the heat and leave to cool for 15 minutes. Whisk the sour cream into the melted chocolate.

Spread one-third of the icing over one cake. Sandwich the other cake on top. Spread the rest of the icing all over the cake. Decorate with sweets and candles.

LEMON POUND CAKE

SERVES 12–16

250 g (9 oz) unsalted butter,
    softened

250 g (9 oz) caster (superfine) sugar

2 teaspoons finely grated lemon zest

1 teaspoon vanilla extract

4 eggs

250 g (9 oz/2 cups) self-raising flour,
    sifted

LEMON BUTTER ICING

60 g (2¼ oz) unsalted butter

125 g (4½ oz/1 cup) icing
    (confectioners') sugar, sifted

2 teaspoons finely grated lemon zest

2 teaspoons lemon juice

Preheat the oven to 180°C (350°F/Gas 4). Grease a deep 20 cm (8 inch) square cake tin and line the base with baking paper.

Beat the butter and sugar with electric beaters until pale and creamy. Beat in the lemon zest and vanilla extract. Add the eggs one at a time, beating until just combined each time. Fold in the sifted flour in two batches until well combined.

Spoon the mixture into the cake tin and bake for 40–50 minutes, or until a skewer inserted into the centre of the cake comes out clean. (Cover the cake loosely with foil if it is browning too quickly.)

Cool the cake in the tin for 10 minutes, before turning out onto a wire rack to cool completely.

To make the lemon butter icing, beat the butter with electric beaters until very soft and white. Beat in the icing sugar, lemon zest and lemon juice.

Spread the icing over the top of the cooled cake.

YOGHURT AND RASPBERRY ICE CREAM

SERVES 4–6

100 g (3½ oz) caster (superfine)
   sugar
500 g (1 lb 2 oz) Greek yoghurt
150 g (5½ oz/1 punnet) raspberries

Whisk the sugar and yoghurt until well combined. Tip the mixture into an ice-cream machine, add the raspberries and churn according to the manufacturer's instructions. This ice cream can become fairly solid, so take it out of the freezer 20 minutes before serving.

CHOCOLATE-CHIP ICE CREAM

SERVES 6–8

100 g (3½ oz) caster (superfine)
   sugar
4 egg yolks
250 ml (9 fl oz/1 cup) milk
150 ml (5 fl oz) cream
1 teaspoon vanilla extract or vanilla
   bean paste
180 g (6 oz) good-quality dark
   chocolate, finely chopped

Whisk the sugar and egg yolks together until thick and pale. Stir in the milk, cream and vanilla extract until well combined. Tip the mixture into an ice-cream machine and churn according to the manufacturer's instructions. Once churned, stir in the chopped chocolate and serve immediately.

COCONUT ICE CREAM

SERVES 6

435 ml (15¼ fl oz/1¾ cups) milk
110 g (3¾ oz/½ cup) caster
   (superfine) sugar
400 ml (14 fl oz) coconut cream

Whisk together the milk and sugar until the sugar has dissolved. Add the coconut cream and mix well. Tip the mixture into an ice-cream machine and churn according to the manufacturer's instructions.

WATERMELON GRANITA

SERVES 10-12

2 kg (4 lb 8 oz) seedless watermelon

110 g (3¾ oz/½ cup) caster (superfine) sugar

3 tablespoons lime juice

Cut the watermelon flesh into bite-sized chunks and place in zip-lock freezer bags. Freeze for 1–2 hours, or until frozen.

Put the frozen watermelon in a food processor and mix until completely smooth. Add the sugar and lime juice and process again until completely incorporated.

Transfer the mixture to an airtight container and freeze for at least 3–4 hours, or until firm.

Once frozen, scrape the granita into crystals with a fork and serve immediately.

"Home-made ice creams are always best when they're freshly churned. We just finish the lot and don't bother saving any for the freezer."

FRUIT JELLY

MAKES 20 SQUARES

1 litre (35 fl oz/4 cups) cranberry or
   pink grapefruit juice
4 tablespoons powdered gelatine
75 g (2½ oz/⅓ cup) caster
   (superfine) sugar (optional)

Put about 250 ml (9 fl oz/1 cup) of the fruit juice in a small bowl and sprinkle the gelatine over the top. Leave until spongy.

Put the rest of the juice in a saucepan over medium heat and add the sugar. Stir until the sugar has dissolved, then add the gelatine and stir until it too has dissolved.

Pour into a 23 cm (9 inch) square tray and refrigerate for 3–4 hours, or until set. Cut into small squares to serve.

FAIRY BREAD

MAKES 12

1½ tablespoons unsalted butter,
   softened
6 thin slices white bread
hundreds and thousands,
   for sprinkling

Butter the bread and sprinkle liberally with hundreds and thousands.

Cut out two hearts from each slice of bread using a 6 cm (2½ inch) cutter.

CHOCOLATE CUSTARD TARTS

MAKES 18

3 egg yolks

55 g (2 oz/¼ cup) caster (superfine) sugar

2 tablespoons cornflour (cornstarch)

1 teaspoon vanilla extract

185 ml (6 fl oz/¾ cup) cream

150 g (5½ oz) dark chocolate, grated

2 sheets frozen puff pastry, thawed

icing (confectioners') sugar, for dusting

Preheat the oven to 220°C (425°F/Gas 7). Lightly grease both a non-stick 6-hole and a 12-hole 125 ml (4 fl oz/ ½ cup) muffin tin.

Place the egg yolks, sugar, cornflour and vanilla extract in a bowl and whisk until smooth. Add the cream and 125 ml (4 fl oz/½ cup) water and whisk again.

Pour the mixture into a saucepan and place over medium heat. Stir for about 5 minutes, or until the mixture is thick. Remove from the heat, add the chocolate and stir until melted. Leave to cool.

Place the puff pastry sheets on top of each other and roll them up. Cut into slices 1 cm (½ inch) wide and roll out into rounds 10 cm (4 inches) in diameter. Push each round into the muffin tin holes. Place in the freezer and chill for 10 minutes.

Divide the cooled custard mixture evenly among the tart shells. Bake for 20 minutes, or until the pastry is golden.

Leave to cool in the tins for 10 minutes before removing. Dust with icing sugar and serve.

INDEX

Published in 2012 by Murdoch Books Pty Limited

Murdoch Books Australia
Pier 8/9
23 Hickson Road
Millers Point NSW 2000
Phone: +61 (0) 2 8220 2000
Fax: +61 (0) 2 8220 2558
www.murdochbooks.com.au
info@murdochbooks.com.au

Murdoch Books UK Limited
Erico House, 6th Floor
93–99 Upper Richmond Road
Putney, London SW15 2TG
Phone: +44 (0) 20 8785 5995
Fax: +44 (0) 20 8785 5985
www.murdochbooks.co.uk
info@murdochbooks.co.uk

For Corporate Orders & Custom Publishing contact Noel Hammond,
National Business Development Manager Murdoch Books Australia

Publisher: Sally Webb
Designer: Emma Gough
Photographer: Petrina Tinslay, with the exception of incidental images on pages 36, 55, 62
from istockphoto library
Stylists: Kristen Anderson, Rebecca Cohen, Kristine Duran-Thiessen, Bill Granger, Marcus Hay,
Michelle Noerianto, and Briget Palmer
Food Editor: Chrissy Freer, Sonia Greig, Lulu Grimes, Jane Lawson, and Jody Vassallo
Copy Editor: Katri Hilden
Project Manager: Kit Carstairs
Production: Joan Beal

National Library of Australia Cataloguing-in-Publication Data
Granger, Bill, 1969-
Bill cooks for kids / Bill Granger.
ISBN 978-1-74266-889-5 (pbk.)
Includes index.
Cooking.
Children--Nutrition.
Cookbooks.
641.5622

A catalogue record for this book is available from the British Library.

Printed by 1010 Printing International Limited, China.

IMPORTANT: Those who might be at risk from the effects of salmonella poisoning (the elderly,
pregnant women, young children and those suffering from immune deficiency diseases)
should consult their doctor with any concerns about eating raw eggs.

OVEN GUIDE: You may find cooking times vary depending on the oven you are using. For fan-forced
ovens, as a general rule, set the oven temperature to 20°C (35°F) lower than indicated in the recipe.